# THE FIRST CHAPBOOK FOR GOLFERS

# THE FIRST CHAPBOOK FOR GOLFERS

*Wit and Wisdom*
*Lessons and Lore*

## COLLECTED AND ANNOTATED BY JEFF SILVERMAN

Woodford Press
Emeryville, CA
2000

Copyright © 2000 by Woodford Press

Printed in the United States.

Edited by Debby Morse.
Book and cover design: Jim Santore, Woodford Press.
Editorial assistance by Nikki Bruno and Shelbey Musso.
Cover illustration by Michel Bohbot.

Library of Congress Card Number: 00-101973
ISBN: 0-942627-66-0

Distributed in the United States and Canada by Andrews McMeel
Publishing, Kansas City, MO

Woodford Press
5900 Hollis Street, Suite K
Emeryville, CA 94608
www.woodfordpub.com

C. David Burgin, Editor and Publisher
Daniel C. Ross, CEO and Publisher
William F. Duane, Senior Vice President

Associate Publishers:

Franklin M. Dumm
William W. Scott
William B. McGuire

# Acknowledgments

With its long history, its considerable roster of heroes, its myriad memorable moments, its psychological trials, and its fairway full of myth, golf tees up a rich and lasting literature as funny, poignant, personal, surprising, exasperating and fulfilling as the very endeavor it attempts to unlock, understand, excuse and explain. Yet, after all the good words set down on the subject by smart and engaging minds, the brilliance of golf's continuing allure remains its essential elusiveness.

No law says we golfers and golf lovers can't have a good time chipping away at it, though. I hope you'll find some forgotten old friends here, be introduced to some new ones, share a few laughs, ponder a few disasters, tap into some inspiration, and pick up a tip or two.

Every book needs a gallery of supporters to see it through, and as the glorified caddie for this one, I'm particularly indebted to Dave Burgin, for a) dreaming up the project, and b) giving me his set of Hogans twenty-some years ago when he desperately needed a golf partner in Paterson, New Jersey.

At Woodford, I'd like to send kudos to Debby Morse, Nikki Bruno, Shelbey Musso, and everyone else for their heavy lifting. I tip my tam to the late *Live!* magazine for paying the freight to golf school, and to Peter Kostis and Gary McCord for making sure I left Grayhawk with at least a nodding acquaintance with the golf swing. Thanks to Chris Hodenfield, Dan Jenkins, Ron Shelton and Bud Shrake for the generosity of their contributions, and to Fred Couples, Ben Crenshaw, Ray Floyd, Richard Mackenzie, and Curt Schilling for the generosity of their time. I'm grateful, in general, to Robert Landau and to Betty

Goodwin, to Keith Klevan for pulling strings, to Harry Cherken and Michael Remington for their counsel, and to Guy Cary for sharing a golf cart. I appreciate Dawn Setzer's research wizardry, Steve Quintavalla's knack for translating physics into English, amazon.com's Lang Cook for helping me build my golf library — and paying me to read the books — and Tom Baldwin for converting one of the world's great used-book stores, Baldwin's Book Barn, into my personal lending library.

And, most of all, I want to thank Abby Van Pelt for altering the course of my solo voyage and making me part of a twosome. She has golf's smoothest backswing, and life's most graceful follow-through; I admit I envy the former, but I benefit from the latter every day.

Jeff Silverman
February 2000

# WHAT IS A CHAPBOOK?

There's not a school-age child in the nation who doesn't know the story of George Washington and the cherry tree; it's part of our national lore. In fact, the fictional tale of the truth-telling boy-who-would-be-president and his axe first appeared in a *chapbook* by Parson Weems.

Dating back to the 16th century, chapbooks were small publications designed for a wide audience of readers, distributed by traveling vendors known as "chapmen." The forerunner of today's magazines and literary reviews, they were practical and affordable, and, unlike their more topical cousins, pamphlets and broadsides, weren't intended to editorialize on what was hot and what was not. Chapbooks contained an assortment of brief texts — sometimes "borrowed" — and were, by nature, timeless. They entertained. They informed. They instructed.

In short, they were the kind of book you could put down, but one you'd be eager to pick up again soon.

There were chapbooks on just about every subject from the deeply sacred to the deliciously profane. Histories were popular, as were biographies, ballads, recipes, household tips, romances, poetry, sermons, anecdotes, and aphorisms, and a rich stew of such genres often appeared in a single-themed volume. Benjamin Franklin wrote and published chapbooks on his own press; in time, he suffused the form with pure American flavor and spun it into *Poor Richard's Almanac.*

As printing costs dropped, chapbooks gave way to larger volumes and magazines. But the concept of an affordable, wide-ranging collection on a specific subject, filled with amusement, trivia, wisdom, and truth, is never dated — hence Woodford's reintroduction of the chapbook, and the birth of a new series of publications.

# CONTENTS

## VIII. THE UN-LIE-ABLE PLAY
### (Etiquette and Sportsmanship)

## IX. CLUBS, COURSES, AND CLUBS
### (The Infrastructure)

## X. DRIVE, HE SAID
### (The How-To's of Golf)

# I

# THE TEXAS TWOSOME

(A COUPL'A GOOD-OLD-BOYS EXPLAIN IT ALL)

*I*

# Harvey Penick and James Michener

### by Bud Shrake

*Author Shrake co-wrote* Harvey Penick's Little Red Book *and three subsequent golf-instruction books with Penick. Phenomenally successful, the books had sold more than three million copies by the beginning of the new century. Shrake wrote this piece for this book.*

On a warm spring afternoon I was sitting in the shade at a table on the east veranda at Austin Country Club with Harvey Penick. We had finished a lunch of tuna salad sandwiches and were drinking iced tea and picking at an hors d'oeuvres platter of raw vegetables and fruits — carrots, radishes, olives, cauliflowers, strawberries, slices of melon. There had been an awful misunderstanding at lunchtime the day before, and I was wishing there was some way I could undo it. Harvey didn't seem bothered in the least, but I was still embarrassed about my part in it.

The misunderstanding was not between Harvey and me, but between Harvey and the famous writer James Michener.

At about this same hour one day earlier, and only a few yards from this same spot, Harvey had met Michener for the first and only time. It was no accidental encounter. I had been the go-between who arranged for them to meet at Austin Country Club. Both men were nearing ninety years of age and were hard of hearing, but they had carried on a loud, lively dialogue, shouting into each other's ears, until that moment I will always regret.

Jim Michener had lived in Austin for years, first in a big house on a hilltop with a view of the city and the river that runs through it but is called a lake, and later in a tidy cottage in the Tarrytown section. He liked the more modest house because it was in a tree-lined neighborhood of small, pleasant lawns, and crackless sidewalks where he enjoyed strolling with his wife, Mari.

Jim and Mari were benefactors of the University of Texas, having donated millions to the school, and were interested in university sports programs, as well. The first time I had met the Micheners was at the Pedernales Country Club — the golf course Willie Nelson owns. The Micheners had recently moved to Austin then. Legendary football coach Darrell Royal and his wife, Edith, took them on an early tour of Austin's most noteworthy places. Willie's golf course was — and still is — high on the agenda of people who know the town best.

The Micheners showed great pleasure and curiosity at the things they were seeing at Willie's — the golfers bounding down the fairways in carts or on foot, the peacock flapping his wings and screeching on the roof of a country clubhouse that had been converted into a recording studio, pool hall and Willie's office.

Being renowned art collectors, the Micheners loved Willie's Bad Art Gallery, a large room full of painted renderings of Willie, usually on black velvet, given to him by fans.

Later I began running into Mari at the small bookstore in Tarrytown. We always stopped to chat. She was a remarkable person, sunny and energetic and smart. Now and then I would see Mari and her husband at some local event. They were warm and cordial, always with that air of friendly curiosity.

I had remarked to Mari one day in the bookstore that she must be a great help to her husband — the kind of innocuous thing you immediately wish you hadn't said. But Mari very seriously replied, "Oh no, not at all. I only keep the household running and the financial matters tended to, and make the travel arrangements so Jim doesn't have to bother with those things. That's all I do. Jim does the writing."

The bookstore closed, alas, and I quit running into Mari except sometimes at the grocery store or with Jim at charity dinners and other gatherings.

Years passed. Harvey asked me to help him get his *Little Red Book* ready for publication. When the book was published, people who had never heard of Harvey were affected by his teachings and his soul as revealed in the heretofore secret notebook that he had kept for sixty years. A subculture that already knew Harvey — including former University of Texas players and such pupils as Betsy Rawls and Kathy Whitworth, among many — at last had an icon of Harvey they could put their hands on and continue to hear his voice.

He spoke through a book with his words in it. *Harvey Penick's Little Red Book* went to number one in *The New York Times*. It became the best-selling sports book in history.

One night came the phone call from Michener, wanting to arrange a meeting with this fascinating man, Harvey Penick. I promised that Harvey would meet him at Austin Country Club, on the east veranda, at 11:30 the following morning. Then I phoned Helen, Harvey's wife, and asked her to tell him. Harvey was too deaf to talk on the phone. Helen told him and I heard him say, "James Michener, the writer?"

"Yes, Harvey."

"What on earth would he want to meet me for?"

"He doesn't want a golf lesson. He just wants to meet you."

"But he's a famous man. Why, he's a very famous writer," Harvey said.

"Don't you want to meet him?" Helen asked.

"Well, sure, I'd like to meet him, but I don't know what I would have to talk about with a famous man like James Michener."

Tacked on my office wall now is a photograph taken the next morning. Harvey is sitting in his golf cart — he could no longer

> "IT IS UTTERLY IMPOSSIBLE FOR ANY GOLFER TO PLAY GOOD GOLF WITHOUT A SWING THAT WILL REPEAT."
> — BEN HOGAN

walk alone — and Jim Michener is sitting beside him. They are parked on the grass east of the veranda, near the door to the men's grill, the Penick Room. Harvey's full figure is etched in glass on the doors into the grill near where the two men sit in the golf cart. They are shouting into each others' hearing aids. Harvey's hearing aid makes squealing noises. Harvey looks eager to communicate but somewhat stifled. Michener has his palms balled atop his walking cane, a big grin on his face and is speaking at a high volume.

I was standing nearby but I couldn't understand a word they said until finally Michener said, "Let's have lunch."

As Michener's assistant was helping him get out of the golf cart, Harvey asked me, "What is he doing?"

"Going to lunch," I said.

Harvey called to his nurse to get behind the wheel of his golf cart. We saw Michener and his assistant opening the glass door with Harvey's picture on it and entering the Penick Room.

"Let's go," Harvey said to his nurse.

"Harvey!" I said. "You're supposed to be eating lunch with Michener."

Harvey nudged his nurse. "I don't think so. Let's go home. I'm hungry. I want a bowl of soup."

"But Harvey!"

The nurse jammed her foot on the pedal, and the golf cart shot away along the side of the clubhouse, past the wall of windows through which those in the men's grill can look out at the grass and trees and water and the putting green, a lovely vision.

Looking out at all those things, his natural curiosity and appreciation for beauty aroused, was the face of James Michener. His eyes widened behind his glasses and his mouth opened in surprise as he saw Harvey speeding away in the golf cart. The nurse turned through the parking lot and the cart whirled along toward Harvey's home a few blocks from the club.

I rushed into the grill. Michener and his assistant sat at a table for four by the window, holding menus. I began to realize what had just happened, but I couldn't bring myself to blurt it in front of the grill room crowd that had its eyes on the visiting celebrity.

Instead, I said I would be back and I hurried out through the front door, shoving open yet another pane with Harvey's figure etched on it. The misunderstanding was Harvey had thought Michener had finished their conversation and now was going to lunch, and it was time for Harvey to make his exit.

Reinforcing Harvey's idea that he had been dismissed was this feeling of his that, although they had named the grill in his honor and had etched his figure on the glass doors, a club golf professional did not belong in the men's grill. For one thing, it involved the old-fashioned caste system of golf under which Harvey grew up. As a young club pro, Harvey was not allowed into the clubhouse. He had to eat at home or in the kitchen.

Later, when strictures against club pros relaxed somewhat, Harvey realized that a club pro could easily get himself into a world of trouble by hanging out in the men's grill. Booze flowed in there, and ideas and opinions were freely and profanely exchanged. Harvey had written to himself in a ledger, "Don't play too much golf or gamble at cards with members. Stay away from the social angles of the club."

He meant it. No men's grill. If I had been alert and had steered Michener and his assistant into the main dining room, Harvey might not have misunderstood that he was not invited to lunch.

I drove to Harvey's home and found him eating vegetable soup in his kitchen. Helen asked me how the meeting with Michener had gone. I said, "Well, it's not supposed to be over yet. Harvey, you need to come back to the club with me and at least sit with Michener. We'll go into the big dining room."

"Aw, thanks, but James Michener is an important man. He doesn't want to have lunch with a teaching pro. He was just being nice," Harvey said.

Harvey said his arthritis was hurting worse than usual and he wanted to sit in his special chair. He wasn't leaving home again today.

Back at the country club, I pushed open Harvey's etched door into the front of the Penick Room. Michener and his assistant had left, the waiter told me. They had looked at their menus for a while and eaten some bread, and then they had thanked everyone and pushed open the Harvey etching on the glass door in back and had disappeared.

"I wish you had come back and had lunch with Michener," I

was saying to Harvey the next day as we sat on the veranda and picked at the platter of vegetables and fruits.

"Now what do you suppose I could have said or done that would be of interest to an important writer like James Michener?" Harvey said.

Just then four Asian men approached our table. One wore a business suit but the others were dressed for golf. They were businessmen from Tokyo who wanted to pay respects to the great Harvey Penick. They had come all this way, they said, to play at the great Austin Country Club that had become famous the world over.

Harvey eyed them closely. The Pete Dye course at Austin Country Club is ferociously difficult. These gentlemen some-how did not carry themselves like golfers who could negotiate the course's many ravines and water hazards. But they said they wanted to play, and from the back tees.

"Which one of you is best?" Harvey asked.

The other three pointed at the man in the suit and tie.

"Let me see your seven-iron," Harvey said.

One of the other gentlemen ran to the bag rack and fetched a club while the man removed his coat, unbuttoned his collar and rolled up his sleeves. He accepted his seven-iron and took up his address.

"Show me your practice swing," Harvey said. The man swung awkwardly, stiff, as though perhaps he had been in an air-plane for eighteen hours.

"I do better with ball," the man said.

They all looked to Harvey for his judgment.

Harvey picked a baby carrot off the hors d'oeuvres tray and tossed the carrot onto the grass at the man's feet.

"Let's see you knock that carrot into that flower bed," Harvey said.

The man lined up his shot.

"No, not at me," Harvey said. "Aim it over thataway."

The man rather awkwardly whacked the carrot in the direction of the flower bed.

"Now? Ball?" he asked.

"Try another carrot," said Harvey.

One by one, each visitor took the seven-iron and knocked all the vegetables from our hors d'oeuvres platter toward the flower bed. Harvey ordered another platter, and they kept at it. Carrots, radishes, cauliflowers, olives, strawberries, melon slices went flying. Some landed in the flowers, but most did not. It was clear by now that this foursome of visitors lacked the golfing skill to make their way around the Pete Dye course before nightfall, if they could ever make it at all. Not only did they look incapable of playing from the back tees, it was doubtful they could even finish the first hole from the men's front tees at the lip of a ravine. I wondered what Harvey was going to do with them now.

After a moment of reflection, Harvey

"IF A GREAT GOLF SWING PUT YOU HIGH ON THE MONEY LIST, THERE'D BE SOME OF US WHO WOULD BE BROKE."
—RAY FLOYD

said, "You need to correct your grips. You'll enjoy the game much more if we adjust your grips. Would each of you, please, step up to my table here? One at a time. With the seven-iron."

For the next few hours Harvey applied himself to each visitor in turn. He moved their hands and their fingers on the handle of the seven-iron. He treated them carefully and courteously, as if each man were as important as any student Harvey had ever met. I could see their faces brighten as Harvey fiddled them into beautiful grips. The visitors were happy and excited. They were being taught by the great man himself. What a story this would be when they got back home.

At last Harvey said, "Now. You've all got good grips. You will play much better golf from now on."

"We go to the first tee now?" asked the man who had shed his suit coat and sweated through his white shirt.

"Oh no," Harvey said. "It's way too soon for you to go to the course. You must practice until you have learned your new grips."

"We don't play today?" asked the man in the dress shirt, disappointed.

"You shouldn't play for at least a week," Harvey said. "Just keep practicing those new grips. Think how much those new grips will improve your games."

The four talked it over in their own language and came to an agreement. They would have to leave Austin before they got to play a round of golf on the Austin Country Club course, but they were more than pleased to have gained knowledge of the grip from the master. Each of them stepped to Harvey's table, bowed, shook his hand and thanked him warmly. Then they hurried away to the driving range, talking and gesturing with delight. This was a wonderful day, an experience they would cherish for the rest of their lives.

Harvey always had his students' best interests at heart. He had saved these visitors from hours of the sort of punishment that Pete Dye golf course architecture can hand out, and he had taught them a fundamental of the game and had made them feel good about themselves at the same time. As I sat there watching and listening, I realized Harvey was enjoying this as much as the four visitors were. I was wishing Michener could have been here to take it in. This was the sort of thing he had been hoping to see Harvey do. I promised myself that the next time I saw Jim Michener I would apologize and tell him this whole story. But our paths never crossed again.

# The Host Club

### by Dan Jenkins

*Jenkins, a former mainstay at* Sports Illustrated, *now writes regularly for* Golf Digest. *In 1999 Woodford Press published* I'll Tell You One Thing, *Jenkins's love letter to college football.*

As a fairly enthusiastic recreational golfer, I was naturally excited when a PGA Tour event came to my country club. I dashed right out there, not only to pick up some swing tips from the pros but to see all of the famous stars in their own flesh and blood and square grooves.

The first shock came when I was forced to park on a school playground five miles away, ride a shuttle bus, and then buy a badge just to get into my own country club. The badge cost $5,000 but the money was for charity, somebody said.

The club sure looked different. A lot of big trucks and mobile homes were sitting around, circus tents had been put up, and a good many wives of members I knew were wearing the same bonnets, blouses, and polka-dot skirts, and were hastily jumping in and out of white Buicks.

"Hi, Mildred," I said. "Where's Fred?"

"I can't talk now," she said, panting. "Mark Brooks needs to go to the dentist and Scott Simpson has to find a discount store." She sped away in the courtesy car.

My next shock came when I entered the clubhouse and a security guard refused to admit me to my own locker room.

"I wish you wouldn't push me in the chest," I said, trying to smile.

"Players and officials only," he said gruffly.

"I am a member," I said.

"Move along, please. Can't you see how crowded this hallway is?"

"I want to use the bathroom," I explained.

The security guard spoke into a walkie-talkie.

"Ralph, we've got a code three in the locker area. Want to send some help down here to get this asshole out? Over."

I got the point and went downstairs to the Men's Grill to grab a bite to eat. There was another security guard on the door.

"Wrong badge," he said, stopping me.

"This is supposed to be good for the clubhouse," I said, fondling the badge pinned to my shirt.

"You're not a Patron."

"A what?"

"Patrons only. Sorry."

"How do you get to be a Patron?" I asked.

"You buy a Patron's badge for ten thousand dollars."

I thought I might find a snack in the Mixed Foursome Room, but, alas, I ran into another security guard.

He shoved me backward.

"My wife and I play bridge in this room," I said.

"You're not a Saint."

"A what?"

"This room is for Saints only."

"What does it cost to be a Saint?"

"I think it's twenty thousand dollars but you get a seat on the eighteenth fairway along with it."

The next place I looked for food was the teenage recreation parlor, which our club calls the Peppermint Lounge.

Yet another security guard was on the door.

I peeked around him and noticed several men and women with cocktails in their hands, while others were loading up their plates at a sumptuous buffet.

"Press only," the security guard said.

"The tournament's outside," I argued.

"They bring the leaders in here to be interviewed," he informed me. "Clear the doorway please. Larry Nelson is on his way here."

It turned out that the only place where a clubhouse badge holder could find food was in the lobby, along with 4,000 other people. I stood in line for two hours and finally got a fat roast beef sandwich and a warm Coke.

"I'll just sign for this," I said when I reached the cashier.

"You need scrip," the lady said.

"I need what?"

"Members can't sign this week. You have to buy scrip. I have a twenty-dollar book for a hundred dollars or a forty-dollar book for 500 dollars."

Giving up on food, I went outside to watch the tournament. At the ninth green, I squeezed into a throng of 10,000 people and caught a glimpse of three golfers down on their hands and knees, evidently staring at insects.

"Which one's Nicklaus?" I asked a fellow spectator.

"Nicklaus doesn't play in this tournament," he said.

Moments later, another group of golfers came to the ninth hole. Mostly, they walked around in circles and held their putters out in front of them, vertically, and squinted.

"Is this Watson?" I inquired.

"Watson never plays here," I was told.

"He doesn't?"

"Naw. Neither does Trevino, or Crenshaw, or Norman, or Zoeller. Palmer plays here, though."

"Great." I said. "When's Arnie coming up?"

"He's not here this year."

I asked which of the famous players were here.

The man said, "Well, that's David Ogrin in the bunker. Bob Lohr's the guy behind the tree trunk. Wayne Grady's waiting on a ruling about the water."

The player I most wanted to watch was Nick Faldo, the greatest golfer in the world. A woman told me she thought Faldo was on the back nine.

I walked out to the fourteenth hole, the farthest point from the clubhouse. There were maybe a dozen fans watching the three players who were identified to me as Tim Simpson, Ronnie Black, and Joe Don Blake.

"I guess Faldo will be coming up pretty soon, huh?" I said to a man sitting under a tree.

"Not this year," the man said. "Faldo can't play in the United States, except in four or five tournaments. Our pros voted on it."

"That's ridiculous," I said, exhausted, hungry, thirsty. "Why am I at this golf tournament if there are no players I've ever heard of?"

"Beats me," the man said. "I'm just sitting here till the goddamn thing's over. The committee closed the street in front of my house and I don't have the right badge to get back home."

# 2
# THE SWEET SPOT

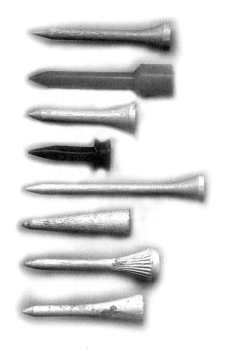

(WHY WE DO THIS)

# Last Evening Light

### by Chris Hodenfield

*We have all played golf courses where the last hole or two will forever remain a mystery, lost in the eternal cloak of darkness. In the fall of 1993, Hodenfield, the editor of* Golf & Travel, *mused in the pages of* Golf Digest *on the quadruple-helix intertwine of the game, the light, the night, and the seasons.*

In Hollywood, the cameramen call it "the golden hour." Only it does not last an hour. It is perhaps twenty minutes of mysterious light that happens when the sun collapses on the horizon.

In golf we have another kind of golden moment that happens sometime after sundown. It is the moment when it occurs to you that you just can't see the ball anymore and you have to stop. Or if you are part of my crowd, you fish through the bag for an old scuffed but serviceable ball and play that one until you lose it.

Even the rattiest old dog track becomes a shining kingdom in sundown's afterglow. The undulations take on a storybook sheen.

This is golf on the edge of night. You play it after work. You play it when you've got kids and this is your only time. You play it when the only course you can get on packs more traffic in peak hours than the Interstate Highway System. You play it when it's the only time you can play. You play it when you just can't stop playing.

You become an expert at gauging the last available light. Looking out the window of the train at the slanting evening sunlight, you think, "Ninety minutes of light. Easy." No one can change shoes faster than a desperate golfer with only an hour's worth of light left. You race to the first tee muttering the usual second-rate prayers: Please let that first tee be empty. Please let there not be any slow, conversation-minded hacks up ahead. The night is coming. Fire up the engines!

If there's a crowd of three-toed sloths up ahead, you might have to skip around from hole to hole. Just keep firing. Finally the gloom pulls in. Other groups are now trudging homeward like battle-weary soldiers returning from war, but you have to keep going. Your sense of perspective flattens out, grows hazy and sharp at the same time. You walk down the dark gray shroud of a shrinking fairway, searching the rough for that bluish white pellet. You arrive at the green and search in vain for a ball. Maybe it's in the cup? The night is exercising its dominion.

\* \* \*

21

There's a sadness that comes in the fall. You're keeping a tireless eye out for the last available light, and like a fool who takes forever to get the joke you notice there's a minute or two less every night. Last August you began to notice it. In September you began to hate it. Now in October it happens — the end of Daylight Savings. Early night. The onslaught of depressions and worse. This is why stock-market collapses happen in autumn. The light — our very life! — is disappearing. Anxieties are on the rise. Who is ready for winter? Not a soul.

But this happens every year! Why does it always come as a glum, miserable surprise that winter is sneaking up on us in a long dark coat? Why do we always feel so freshly shell-shocked on that early November evening when we step outside after work and notice it's dark already? With the bare-trees chilling of winter so close at hand, and a sense of gloom hanging over you like a Swedish movie, you realize: there is no sense heading for the course for a fast nine. There will not even be any short-game practice tonight.

At a time like this, even miniature golf wouldn't be that disgraceful. Because that's all you're going to get tonight.

Scientists have come up with any number of impressive names for the woes of winter. They call it SAD — Seasonal Affective Disorder. They tell us we are depressed because not enough full-spectrum sunlight enters our eyeballs. We could have told them that. How else could we tolerate the game of golf? No matter how we slop the ball around, all that full-spectrum light entering our eyeballs makes us feel warm. That may in fact be the whole reason we play golf. Surely it can't be the scores.

In winter, the light must be treasured. We must go outside at noontime to bask in just a few moment's sunshine. In dark times you must join hands with the Aztec sun-worshippers. You have to search for the sun with the ferocious drive of a buried coal miner who sees a trickle of light in a far-off crevice.

Civilization has engineered all these winter social substitutes to get us through the dark season, feasts such as Thanksgiving, Fasching, Christmas, Hanukkah, New Year's, the Super Bowl. Holidays so enchanting you now need a pocketful of Valium to get through them in one piece. Call it what you will — winter-depressive, spectrum-impoverished, suntan-challenged, whatever — it all adds up to a case of the blues. Playing some computer golf game will not fill the eyes with light. The simplest remedy might be a trip to Argentina.

But there's hope. Haven't you noticed that the day after New Year's brings considerable relief?

... By the end of January, the light is beginning to last just that necessary little bit longer in the day. You hit the bricks in the evening and there may be a moment's glow waiting. It's a light that holds promise. After a few false starts, setbacks, rain delays and muddy days, you will be out in the wide space again, firing away.

Some people confess that they regard sundown as an hour of unendurable melancholy. Day or night is fine, but anything in between wracks their nerves. They talk like people coming down hard from too many cups of coffee.

Of course there is an emotional twinge at the end of the day. That's why you have to be walking around outside as the whole earth exhales and offers you one last look. You hear the birds settle down and sense the mist rising. Meandering down an abandoned fairway, you try hard not to believe that there is anything richly symbolic about poking around in the long grass for a lost ball. Any game that lets you say goodbye to the day like this has to be a noble game.

*"Gotta run, sweetheart. By the way, that was one fabulous job you did raising the children."*

# The Mystery of Golf

### by Arnold Haultain

*Canadian belle-lettrist Haultain (1857-1941) came to golf in mid-life and approached the game analytically with a convert's fascination and zeal. John Updike, who has produced his share of titanium prose on the subject, deemed the core of Haultain's* The Mystery of Golf, *quietly published in an edition of 400 in 1908, "pure gold." A pair of nuggets ensues.*

Three things there are as unfathomable as they are fascinating to the masculine mind: metaphysics; golf; and the feminine heart. The Germans pretend to have solved some of the riddles of the first, and the French to have unraveled some of the intricacies of the last; will some one tell us wherein lies the extraordinary fascination of golf?

I have just come home from my Club. We played till we could not see the flag; the caddies were sent ahead to find the balls by the thud of their fall; and a low large moon threw whispering shadows on the dew-wet grass or ere we trode the home-green. At dinner the talk was of golf; and for three mortal hours after dinner the talk was — of golf. Yet the talkers were neither idiots, fools, nor monomaniacs. On the contrary, many of them were grave men of the world. At all events the most monomaniacal of the lot was a prosperous man of affairs, worth I do not know how many thousands, which thousands he had made by the same mental faculties by which this evening he was trying to probe or to elucidate the profundities and complexities of this so-called "game." Will someone tell us wherein lies its mystery?

* * *

All true games ... are contests. But in golf the contest is not with your fellow man. The foe in golf is not your opponent, but great Nature herself, and the game is to see who will overreach her better, you or your opponent. In almost all other games you pit yourself against a mortal foe; in golf it is yourself against the world: no human being stays your progress as you drive your ball over the face of the globe. It is very like life in this, is golf. Life is not an internecine strife. We are all here fighting, not against each other for our lives, but against Nature for our livelihoods. In golf we can see a symbol of the history and fate of humankind: careering over the face of this open earth, governed by rigid rule, surrounded with hazards, bound to subdue Nature or ere we can survive, punished for the minutest divergence from the narrowest course, and the end of it all.... And the end of it all?... To reach an exiguous grave with as few mistakes as may be — some with high and brilliant flight, others with slow and lowly crawl....

# Keep Your Eye On the Ball

## by *Grantland Rice*

*A defining keyboard artist of the Golden Age of American sportswriting, Henry Grantland Rice (1880-1954) was also an avid duffer and master of doggerel. He offered this verse as the rallying rhyme for St. Andrews Golf Club in Hastings-on-Hudson, New York.*

Boy, if the phone should ring,
  Or anyone come to call,
Whisper that this is spring —
  To come again next fall.
Say I have a date on a certain tee
Where my friends the sand-traps wait in glee;
Tell them the 'Doc' has ordered me
  To keep my eye on the ball.

Boy, if they wish to know
  Where I shall haunt the scene,

27

Tell them to leave and go
   Out by the ancient green.
Tell them to look where the traps are deep
And the sand flies up in a powdered heap,
And out of the depths loud curses creep
   To the flash of a niblick sheen.

Then if the boss should sigh,
   Or my presence seek,
Tell him the truth, don't lie;
   Say that my will was weak.
For what is a job to a brassie shot
That whistles away to an untrapped spot,
Or the thrill of a well-cut mashie shot,
   Or the sweep of a burnished cleek?

# Kipling Courageous

While there's no hard evidence as to rain and sleet, snow certainly never stayed Rudyard Kipling from his appointed rounds. At least not after necessity led him to discover the usefulness of painting golf balls red.

Between 1892 and 1896, the prolific writer and his wife settled in on an eleven-acre estate in Brattleboro, Vermont. Naturally, his clubs, including one fashioned by the hands of Old Tom Morris, accompanied him for the duration. Writing in the morning, Kipling penned his beloved classics *The Jungle Books* and *Captains Courageous* here. In the afternoon, he played golf.

The game was in its American infancy then, and both courses and golfing partners were scarce. Kipling used his ingenuity to solve the first problem; he played a makeshift layout of indeterminate par that extended from the meadow beyond his front door right to the edge of the Connecticut River. As for fellow golfers, his most noted companion was *Sherlock Holmes* mastermind Sir Arthur Conan Doyle, who visited in 1894. Doyle apparently had as good a knack for solving golf's mysteries as he did Holmes's cases; he gave Kipling lessons during his stay.

But it was Kipling's most frequent links companion, the Rev. Charles O. Day of the local Congregationalist Church, who chronicled the tale of how he and Kipling ultimately triumphed over the obvious — and not so obvious — hazards of golf in New England:

"We played golf over snow two feet deep, upon the crust," he wrote in 1899, "cutting holes in the snow and naturally losing the balls, until it occurred to [Kipling] to ink them red. The first day we experimented with them, we dyed the plain like some football gridiron; then we had them painted.

"The trouble with golfing on the crust was that, as the meadow was upon a sidehill with gradual slope, a ball went on forever unless headed off by some kindly stone wall or by one's opponent. It was an easy matter to make a drive of two miles.

"As spring came, little 'putting greens' emerged like oases in the snow, and then we had holes made of empty vegetable cans sunk in the moist soil. For a touch of courtesy, I recollect his intentional miss of a hole one inch away, throwing a victory to me, who was a stroke and five yards behind him.

"Retiring from outdoor sports, we would repair to the library for tea and talk…. His play was good, but his dramatic description immensely better."        —J. S.

# A Diversion in the Fields Called the Links

### by *Tobias Smollett*

*Doctor-turned-writer Smollett (1721-1771) rests securely in the pantheon of important 18th-century masters of fiction. With this passage from his final book,* The Expedition of Humphry Clinker, *he deserves a spot in the Golf Writers Hall of Fame as well; it's the first incorporation of golf's existence in a novel. Once a man of medicine, always a man of medicine, and Smollett was naturally high on what he perceived to be the game's restorative powers.*

Hard by, in the fields called the Links, the citizens of Edinburgh divert themselves at a game called Golf, in which they they use a curious kind of bats tipped with horn, and small elastic balls of leather, stuffed with feathers, rather less than tennis balls, but of a much harder consistence. These they strike with such force and dexterity from one hole to another that they will fly to an incredible distance. Of this diversion the Scots are so fond, that, when the

"AS IN BILLIARDS, MAKE EACH SHOT WITH A DEFINITE VIEW AS TO THE NEXT ONE."
— HORACE HUTCHINSON

weather will permit, you may see a multitude of all ranks, from the senator of justice to the lowest tradesman, mingled together, in their shirts, and following the balls with the utmost eagerness. Among others, I was shown one particular set of golfers, the youngest of whom was turned of four-score. They were all gentlemen of independent fortunes, who had amused themselves with this pastime for the best part of a century, without having ever felt the least alarm from sickness or disgust; and they never went to bed without having each the best part of a gallon of claret in his belly. Such uninterrupted exercise, cooperating with the keen air from the sea, must, without all doubt, keep the appetite always on edge, and steel the constitution against all the common attacks of distemper.

# The Greatest Shot
# Ever Landed

For sheer bravura, nerve and creative application of local knowledge, it would be hard to match the display of former British Boys Champion and 1935 Open qualifier Laddie Lucas. But then, he had certain advantages right from the tee.

He was born, in 1915, Percy Belgrave Lucas in the clubhouse overlooking the first fairway of Prince's Golf Club in Sandwich, just north of Dover; his father co-founded the club, and the family lived on the premises. Encouraged by his father, he developed into the best left-handed British amateur of his era. He made his Walker Cup debut in 1936; eleven years later, he captained the team.

His greatest shot came in between, however, when German aircraft attacked — and damaged — the Spitfire he was piloting on a mission over France.

It was late in World War II, and Lucas's dashing reputation as one of the RAF's most celebrated aces had already been established. What followed raised his legend from mere decorated fighter pilot into linksland myth.

*33*

Despite being hit, Lucas managed to get himself — and his unit — out of French territory and over the Strait of Dover. Halfway across, his engine died. He had no alternative, he thought, than to aim for the water and take the penalties.

Then...

"Suddenly through the haze," he recalled years later, "away to the north ... I could see the faint outline of Prince's Clubhouse. It's prophetic, I thought." His only hope was to keep aloft long enough to try putting down, within view of his old nursery window, on that very familiar — and flat — first fairway.

"True to all known form," he relayed as only a golfer would, "I missed the first fairway, the second, the sixth and the eighth, and finished up out of bounds in the marsh at the back of the old ninth green."

It was certainly the best miss of a long and distinguished career.

Lucas remained close to the game for the rest of his life. After a decade in Parliament, he was present at the creation of the European Tour in the early '70s, and up to the day he died in 1998, he was still quite proudly active as vice president of both the British Golf Foundation and the Association of Golf Writers.                —J. S.

# 3

# GOLF SPELLED
# BACKWARDS IS "FLOG"

(WHY DO WE DO THIS?)

# An Unlucky Golfer

### by A. A. Milne

*Alan Alexander Milne (1882-1956) is, of course, more associated with Pooh Corner than Amen Corner. He would be the first to admit, as he does here, that the golf world is quite fortunate it wasn't the other way around.*

I am the world's unluckiest golfer. Yes, I know what you are going to say, but I don't mean what you mean. Of the ordinary bad luck which comes to us all at times I do not complain. It is the "rub of the green." When my best drive is caught by cover, or fielded smartly by mid-on with his foot; when I elect to run a bunker ten yards away and am most unfortunately held up by blown sand (or, as I generally call it, dashed sand); when I arrive at last on the green, and my only hope of winning the hole is that my opponent shall pick up a worm which he ought to have brushed away, or brush away one which he ought to have picked up... and there are no worms out that morning; on all these occasions I take my ill-luck with a shrug of the shoulders and something as nearly like a smile as I can manage. After all, golf would be a very dull game if it were entirely a matter of skill.

It is in another way altogether that I am singled out by Fate. Once I have driven off the first tee, she is no more unkind to me than to the others. By that time she has done her worst. But sometimes it is as much as I can do to get onto the first tee at all, so relentless is her persecution of me. Surely no other golfer is so obstructed.

I suppose my real trouble is that I take golf too seriously. When I arranged many years ago to be at St. Margaret's at 2:30 on Wednesday, I was at St. Margaret's at 2:30 on Wednesday. I didn't ring up suddenly and say that I had a cold, or that my dog wanted a run, or that a set of proofs had just arrived which had to be corrected quickly. No, I told myself that an engagement was an engagement. "Wednesday, St. Margaret's, 2:30" — I turned up, and have never regretted it. If today my appointment is "Sunningdale, Thursday, 10:45," it is as certain that I shall be there. But these other golfers, one wonders how they ever get married at all.

I am not saying that they are careless about their promises; not all of them; but that, in their case, the mere fact of making an important appointment seems to bring out something: spots or a jury-summons or a new baby. I suppose that, when they play with each other, they hardly notice these obstructions, for if A has to plead an unexpected christening on the Monday, B practically knows that he will have to have his tonsils removed suddenly on the Thursday, when the return match is to be played; wherefore neither feels resentment against the other. Only I, who take golf seriously, am surprised. "Tonsils, juries, christenings," I say to myself; "but I thought we were playing golf."

But not only am I a serious golfer; I am, as I have said, the world's unluckiest one. The most amazing things happen to the people who arrange to play with me. On the very morning of our game they are arrested for murder, summoned to Buckingham Palace, removed to asylums, sent disguised to Tibet, or asked to play the leading part in Hamlet at twenty-four hours' notice. Any actor out of work would be wise to fix up a game with me, for on that day he would almost certainly be sent for to start rehearsing. Of course, he might have a fatal accident instead, but that is a risk which he would have to take.

However, it is time that you saw my golf in action. Here, then, is a typical day, unexaggerated.

On a certain Wednesday I was to play a couple of rounds with a friend. On Tuesday afternoon I rang him up on the telephone to remind him of our engagement, and in the course of a little talk before we hung our receivers up, I said that I had just been lunching with an actor-manager, and he said that he had just been bitten by a mosquito. Not that it mattered to the other in the least, but one must have one's twopennyworth.

Wednesday dawned, as it has a habit of doing, but never did it dawn so beautifully as now; the beginning of one of those lovely days of early autumn than which nothing is more lovely. That I was to spend this whole beautiful day playing golf, not working, was almost too good to be believed. I sang as I climbed into my knickerbockers; I was still singing as I arranged the tassels of my garters.... And, as I went down to breakfast, the telephone bell began to sing.

I knew at once, of course. With all the experience I have had, I knew. I merely wondered whether it was the man himself who was dead, or one of his friends.

"Hallo," said his voice. So he was alive.

"Yes?" I said coldly.

"Hallo! I say, you remember the mosquito?" (Which mosquito?) "Well, my leg is about three times its ordinary size." (Does that matter? I thought. None of us is really symmetrical.) "I can hardly move it... Doctor... Nurses... Amputate... In bed for a year..." He babbled on, but I was not listening; I was wondering if I could possibly find somebody else.

It is a funny thing, but somehow I cannot write in knickerbockers. Once I have put them on I find it impossible to work. I must play golf. But alas! how difficult to find another at such short notice. As a last hope I decided to ring up Z. Z is almost as keen a golfer as myself. No such trifle as a lack of uniformity in his legs would keep him from his game. I cut off the other fellow as he was getting to the middle of his third operation, and got on to Z. Z, thank Heaven for him, would play.

I called for him. We drove down. We arrived. With each succeeding minute the morning became more lovely; with each succeeding minute I thanked Heaven more for Z. As we walked over to the caddiemaster I was almost crying with happiness.

> "GOLF IS NOT A FUNERAL, BUT BOTH CAN BE SAD AFFAIRS."
> — BERNARD DARWIN

Never was there a day more beautiful. All this mosquito business had made us late, and there were no caddies left, but did I mind? Not a bit! On a morning like this, I thought to myself as I stepped on to the first tee, I couldn't mind anything.

The moment that Z stepped onto the first tee, I knew that I was mistaken. You will never believe it, but I give you my word that it is true. Z stepped on to the wrong bit of the first tee, uttered one loud yell… and collapsed on the grass with a broken ankle.

You say that I might have left him there and played a few holes by myself? I did. But it was necessary to give instructions for him to be removed before others came after me. I forget the exact rule about loose bodies on the tee, but a fussy player might easily have objected. So I had to go back and tell the secretary, and one way and another I was delayed a good deal. And of course it spoiled my day entirely.

But I was not surprised. As I say, I am the world's unluckiest golfer.

# How to Make
# a Hole in Nine

### by Grantland Rice

*Among the treasures proudly displayed in his great friend Bobby Jones's office was a personalized print of Rice's most enduring lines of verse: "For when the one great scorer comes to mark against your name/He writes — not that you won or lost — but how you played the game." A fine player, he took the helm of* The American Golfer *in 1919 and steered the course of that truly sophisticated sporting journal for nearly twenty years. He published his droll* A Duffer's Handbook of Golf, *which included this all-too-familiar recipe for disaster, in 1926.*

While making a hole in nine is not one of the most difficult of all the golfing arts, it is not as simple as many may think it to be. Yet if one follows instructions carefully it can be accomplished with fair consistency.

The surest way is to miss a short putt on the preceding green and then advance to the next tee thinking about that missed short putt while applying to the game of golf in general every known epithet that one can remember. Continue to brood over that missed putt and to think about it exclusively as you lash at your tee shot with a tight grip and a fast backswing. You will probably drive the first ball out of bounds and top the next attempt into the rough. Then, without calming or soothing your flaming soul, slash away at your recovery shot in about the same way. You can now be thinking about the out-of-bounds and the topped drive as well as the short missed putt. Think of everything you can except the next stroke to be played.

By your fourth stroke you will probably be in a heel print in some deep pit. This is an ideal situation for the hole-in-nine result. Curse the heel print, bawl out fate, destiny, and Scotland, grip your niblick with the clutch of doom and hammer away. This should put you on the green in six. The next few steps are easy. In place of settling down, continue to boil over and rap the first putt with a savage disregard of distance or direction. This should put you about twelve feet past the cup. Your next putt will be about three feet short or over. This will be eight. The final move is to hit the ball carelessly with one hand as you pick it up and concede yourself the nine. Don't make the mistake at any time of relaxing or concentrating on the next stroke to be played. This may cut off two or more strokes.

# A Golfer's Wish

### *by Edgar Guest*

*Dubbed "The Poet of the People," Guest (1881-1959) published a poem a day — something like 11,000 of them — during his thirty-year run as a columnist for the* Detroit Free Press. *Much of his work was inspirational, even sappy, but not even he could surgarcoat failure on the golf course.*

I have no wish to dress in silk,
   I do not care to wear a crown,
I do not yearn to bathe in milk,
   Or champagne wash my dinner down.

I have no great desire to be
   A man of much importance here,
And have the public welcome me
   With bands of brass when I appear.

And should a fairy, kind and good,
   Grant me one favor, without price,

*43*

I'd make this golfer's prayer, I would:
"Oh, kindly rid me of my slice!"

I am not one intent on fame;
I do not care to lead the throng;
Though strangers never hear my name,
Contentedly I'll plod along.

Enough to eat, enough to wear,
And strength to do my daily task,
With now and then a chance to fare
On pleasure's ways, is all I ask.

But should a fairy come to me
And say: "What joy will you suffice?
I'll grant one wish. What shall it be?"
I'd answer: "Rid me of my slice!"

You that have never swung a club
And drawn its face across the ball,
And muttered to yourself, "You dub!"
As in a curve you watched it fall,

May never guess the rage that lies
Within that shortened arc of flight,
Nor how men curse the fall that flies
With loss of distance, to the right.

But every golfing fiend will know
    Why gold and fame I'd sacrifice,
If but some fairy, good, would show
    Me how to drive without a slice.

# The Most Absorbing Game

### by A. J. Balfour

*It's hard to imagine Arthur James Balfour (1848-1930) having time to play golf let alone write so eloquently about it, even if he was Scottish born. But then the first Earl of Balfour was a remarkable man on several counts: historian, philosopher, and statesman. First elected to the House of Commons in 1874, he served Great Britain as Prime Minister from 1902 to 1905, and later led the mission that issued the 1917 declaration, bearing his name, announcing Britain's support of the creation of a homeland for the Jews in Palestine. He contributed these splendid observations in an essay titled* The Humours of Golf *to Hutchinson's* Badminton Library *volume on the game.*

It is hard that a game which seems to those who do not play it to be so meaningless should be to those who do play it not only the most absorbing of existing games, but occasionally in the highest degree irritating to the nerves and to the temper. The fact itself will, I apprehend, hardly be denied, and the reason I suppose to be this, that as in most games action is rapid and more or less unpremeditated, failure seems less humiliating in itself, and there is less time to brood over it.

In most games — e.g. cricket, tennis, football — effort succeeds effort in such quick succession that the memory of particular blunders is immediately effaced or deadened. There is leisure neither for self-examination nor for repentance. Even good resolutions scarce have time to form themselves, and as soon as one difficulty is surmounted, mind and body have to brace themselves to meet the next. In the case of golf it is far otherwise. The player approaches his ball with every circumstance of mature deliberation. He meditates, or may meditate, for as long as he pleases on the precise object he wishes to accomplish and the precise method by which it may best be accomplished. No difficulties are made for him by his opponent; he has no obstacles to overcome but those which are material and inanimate.

Is there not, then, some natural cause for irritation when, after every precaution has been taken to insure a drive of 150 or 180 yards, the unfortunate player sees his ball roll

AND THE WIND SHALL SAY: "HERE WERE DECENT GODLESS PEOPLE/ THEIR ONLY MONUMENT THE ASPHALT ROAD/ AND A THOUSAND LOST GOLF BALLS."

— T. S. ELIOT, THE ROCK

47

gently into the bottom of a bunker some twenty yards in front of the teeing ground and settle itself with every appearance of deliberate forethought at the bottom of the most inaccessible heel mark therein? Such an event brings with it not merely disaster, but humiliation; and, as a last aggravation, the luckless performer has ample leisure to meditate over his mishap, to analyze its causes, to calculate the precise effects which it will have on the general fortunes of the day, and to divine the secret satisfaction with which his opponent has observed the difficulties in which he has so gratuitously involved himself.

No wonder that persons of irritable nerves are occasionally goaded to fury. No wonder that the fury occasionally exhibits itself in violent and eccentric forms....

# The Golfer's Prayer

*by Ring Lardner*

I do not ask for strength to drive
   Three hundred yards and straight;
I do not ask to make in five
   A hole that's bogey eight.

I do not want a skill in play
   Which others can't attain;
I plead but for one Sunday
   On which it doesn't rain.

# 4

## GET A GRIP

(THE PSYCHOLOGY OF THE GAME)

# Joyce Wethered's One-Track Mind

Bobby Jones once described the straight-hitting Joyce Wethered as the best golfer with the best swing he'd ever seen — period. "I have not played golf with anyone, man or woman, amateur or professional, who made me feel so utterly outclassed," he wrote following

a round with her at St. Andrews in 1930 just prior to his victory in the British Amateur.

But if her swing was good, her focus was better. Ten years before playing with Jones, she reached the final match of the first Ladies' British Open Amateur Championship that she would play in — at the Sheringham Golf Club on the Norfolk coast. On the seventeenth green, as she was preparing to take what would turn into the crucial putt of the match, a train thundered by on the adjacent tracks. Not missing a beat, she holed the putt and went on to win the first of her five consecutive Ladies' titles.

When asked after the match whether the train had bothered her concentration, she responded — in true championship form — "What train?"                    —J. S.

# A Snapshot in Time: Fred Couples

### by *Jeff Silverman*

oom!

Freddie Couples, the matinee idol of golf, has just three-putted for bogey from the fringe off the eighteenth at Riviera, so...

Boom!

... Freddie Couples, despite a blistering 67 in the penultimate round of the 1993 Los Angeles Open, has lost a stroke that minutes before had seemed safer than an insured deposit. The coolest cucumber on the fairway still has a share of the lead — he would lose it the next day to Tom Kite — but he isn't happy. You might just say he's teed off.

Boom!

This is a condition barely visible to the naked eye. It's not as if he's breaking brassies over his knee or howling curses to the breezes. His face isn't wracked with pain. No. That wouldn't be Fred Couples, a.k.a. the carefree couch potato of professional sports; the phlegmatic enigma with the effortless swing and the effortless walk and the effortless style but no goals, no direction, no emotions and less internal drive than an electric cart on drained batteries; an athlete so laid-back it's a wonder he doesn't tip over; a fellow who's been known to explain — when he has the energy to finish a sentence — that he doesn't pick up a ringing telephone because there's probably someone at the other end. But, as he tends to his post-round business on Riviera's practice range…

Boom!

… the sound of self-flagellation is unmistakable. Here, driver in grasp, the winner of this tournament in 1990 and '92, and reigning PGA Player of the Year two years running, can can give the slip to the pullers and pokers, the idolators, the well-wishers, the questioners, the suggesters, the naysayers, the glad-handers, the autograph hounds, the divorce lawyers and the missed putts — oh, those missed putts! Here, protected by the Maginot Line of a yellow rope, he can do what he has a knack for doing better than just about anyone else on the planet: shutting out the world, unsheathing golf's smoothest and most rhythmically fluid swing, beating some balls and, in his own stoic way, beating back the frustrations of the most frustrating game ever conjured by evil Druids.

> "THE TWO QUALITIES THAT HELP ME THE MOST: HONESTY ABOUT MY WEAKNESSES AND A SENSE OF HUMOR. DON'T TRY SHOTS BEYOND ONE'S ABILITY, AND DON'T GET UPSET ON THE COURSE."
> — JOYCE WETHERED

The sounds of the tensions and pressures...

Boom!

... of a stroke handed back to the field on a less-than-silver putter in a year that has begun neither personally nor professionally...

Boom!

... on quite a par with the annus mirabilis that came before...

Boom!

... are audible in the whip and impact of every gracefully perfect swing. Unfocused? Unemotional? Directionless? Carefree? Hell, the way Freddie's on attack...

Boom!

... they can probably feel the reverb...

Boom!

... in Hawaii.

"I will lay it on the line," Couples would tell me several months later when I reminded him of that missed putt and the turbocharged display that followed, of a man possessed and a ball to take it out on. "I think golf can really make you mental. I just hate making mistakes, giving away shots. It can really cause problems. Other than that" — a smile too cherubic for any human being of thirty-three to form quickly steadies the yips of an off-line memory — "I think it's pretty easy."

Yeah. Easy for him to say.

Boom!

—J. S.

# We Can't All Be Idiots

## by Sir Walter Simpson

*When Simpson (1843-1898) published his classic* The Art of Golf *in 1887, he staked his claim as the game's first psychologist — or at least the first to explore the lunar landscape of the golfer's mind and conclude his subject had rocks in the head.*

Excessive golfing dwarfs the intellect. And this is to be wondered at when we consider that the more fatuously vacant the mind is, the better for play. It has long been observed that absolute idiots ignorant whether they are playing two more or one off two, play steadiest. An uphill game does not make them press, nor victory within their grasp render them careless. Alas! We cannot all be idiots. Next to the idiotic, the dull, the unimaginative mind is the best for golf. In a professional competition I would prefer to back the sallow, dull-eyed fellow with a "quid" in his cheek, rather than any more eager-looking champion. The poetic temperament is the worst for golf. It dreams of brilliant drives, iron shots laid dead, and long putts held, whilst in real golf success waits for him who takes care of the foozle and leaves the fine shots to take care of themselves.

# Of Yippers, Twitchers and Jitterers

### by Peter Dobereiner

*A staple on the pages of the* Observer, *the* Manchester Guardian, *and* Golf Digest, *Dobereiner (1926-1996) filled his golfing dispatches with droll charm and wry wit. He could be as majestic writing about Hogan conquering Carnoustie as he was sardonic here, in the* Observer *in 1984, writing about how the yips, in turn, ultimately conquered Ben.*

Apart from being beaned by errant golf balls, assaulted by peevish golfers who resent being described in print as choppers, incurring curvature of the spine through being cramped up in cheap charter flights and suffering lurid stomach disorders from foreign cuisine, the main occupational hazards of the golf correspondent are scrivener's palsy and writer's block.

You don't want to hear about my problems. You have

troubles of your own. But wait. Scrivener's palsy is out to get all of us who play golf. Otherwise known as writer's cramp, it afflicts the pen-holding hand with a rigor which precludes any function more legible than the trail of a drunken spider which has fallen into the ink pot. The palsy in turn induces writer's block, a condition which turns the patient into a dull-eyed zombie who sits staring for hours at a blank sheet of paper and cursing the biological bulldozer which has severed all lines of communication to the brain.

The same fate awaits golfers, which is why I am glad to see that medical science is at last taking this form of hysteria with due seriousness in the person of Dr. Wolfgang Schady, consultant-lecturer in neurology at Manchester University. He has just addressed the British Association on the subject known variously as the Yips, the Twitch, the Staggers, the Waggles, the Jitters, or just Them.

The Twitch apparently is one of a group of disorders known as occupational cramps, and victims include violinists, telegraphists and, frightful thought, milkers. "Hold on, Daisy. I'll just do some finger-flexing exercises and we'll try again."

The late Henry Longhurst was a sufferer from the Twitch, and the experience of taking three putts from a yard on the eighteenth green at St. Andrews was the final indignity which caused him to give up the game which he had graced and loved all his life.

> "REMEMBER, THIS GAME WAS INVENTED BY THE SAME PEOPLE WHO THINK GOOD MUSIC COMES FROM BAGPIPES."
> — SIGN ON A CHICAGO AREA GOLF COURSE

He wrote what I have always considered to be the definitive description of the Yip Syndrome, with a grim catalogue of case histories. Thus Tommy Armour: "That ghastly time when, with the first movement of the putter, the golfer blacks out, loses sight of the ball and hasn't the remotest idea of what to do with the putter or, occasionally, that he is holding a putter at all."

Or Harry Vardon, who once lost the U.S. Open by missing a one-inch putt: "As I stood addressing the ball I would watch for my right hand to jump. At the end of two seconds I would not be looking at the ball at all. My gaze would have become riveted on my right hand. I simply could not resist the desire to see what it was going to do. Directly, as I felt that it was about to jump, I would snatch at the ball in a desperate effort to play the shot before the involuntary movement could take effect. Up would go my head and body with a start and off would go the ball, anywhere but on the proper line."

The Twitch has ended the career of many a good man. Wild Bill Mehlhorn was finished after he jerked a three-footer clear across the green into a bunker. Craig Wood finally had to accept that perseverance was useless against this destructive malady. Peter Alliss was one of the most gifted players I have ever seen, up to about five feet from the hole. Those last few excruciating inches did for him when he was in his prime, prematurely ending his distinguished career. The same goes double for Ben Hogan.

Many remedies have been tried but mostly they proved to be no more than palliatives. Leo Diegel's spread-elbow style merely postponed the inevitable. Cross-handed grips, spread-handed styles, often with the right hand down on the hosel, one-handed with twelve-inch putters, index finger down the shaft ... and putting with the eyes closed have all been advocated from time to time.

Sam Snead, among others, found a new lease on golfing life with the croquet method until the United States Golf Association banned standing astride the line of the putt. Snead adapted the croquet method with his sidewinder style, not with outstanding success but at least it enabled him to make a controlled stroke.

Armour theorized that the Yips were a tournament disease, the result of years of competitive strain which produced a sort of punch-nuttiness with the putter. Longhurst challenged that conclusion, rightly pointing out that the disorder was common among ordinary club golfers who never played serious competitive golf.

Where I take issue with Longhurst is in his bleak conclusion that "Once you've had 'em, you've got 'em," and I am encouraged in this opinion by Dr. Schady, despite the fact that a member of his department at Manchester has developed a pen which delivers an electric shock whenever scrivener's palsy sets in.

"Such Pavlovian methods have not been used on golfers afflicted with the Yips, perhaps because an electrified golf club sounds vaguely threatening [I love that 'vaguely'] and would probably be illegal."

Nevertheless there is hope, as the example of Bernhard Langer shows. As a teenager he had the worst case of Yips I have ever seen and yet today he is at the top of the European Tour's putting statistics with an average below 30. This is the man who used to rejoice on the rare occasions when he did not have a four-putt green in his round.

One cause of the Yips, I am convinced, is that some golfers' vision of the hole does not coincide with its actual position. They are always aiming at a target which isn't there. Langer, for instance, has severe astigmatism in one eye and he has at last learned to lay off his aim to accommodate the disorder, directing his putts at a phantom hole, in truth the real hole, wide of the one he sees.

If an eye test fails to cure the Yips, then Dr. Schady's advice to use a different technique is sound, so far as it goes. My conclusion is that the Twitch afflicts the small muscles of the fingers and hands and that salvation lies in taking them out of the action. Clamp the arms to the side and immobilize the hands and wrists on the grip. Now move the club head with a lateral shimmy of the hips. It looks odd, as if Twitchers care about that, but it does work. And once the short putts start to drop regularly, normal service is gradually restored to the hands and the patient can return to his normal method. Try it; you have nothing to lose but the match.

# Upon Winning One's Flight in the Senior Four-Ball

### by John Updike

Oh, where have they gone to — the eight-iron stiff to the pin,
after two less fortunate shots, setting up a par;
the calmly stroked putt that snatched a win away
from the staggered opponents; the heroic long drive
that cleared the brook on the fly by a foot or two;
the bravely slashed wedge that lifted the plugged ball
up in a sea-spray of sand to bobble gamely toward the hole?

How can these feats matter so little, so soon after
they mattered so much? The blood thrumming in the temples,
the rushes of love for one's doughty, erratic partner,
the murderous concentration upon imaginary
abstractions carved in the air by sheer sinew and bond —
boiled down to a trinket of silver, a tame patter
of applause in the tent, a pleasantry, a kind of loss.

# 5
# THE LEADERBOARD

(LEGENDS OF GOLF)

# The Ultimates

## The Ultimate Golf Tip

"Nobody ever swung a golf club too slowly."
—*Bobby Jones*

## The Ultimate Golf Tribute

It seems only fitting that Jones would receive the game's ultimate final tribute. When word of his death reached the Old Course at St. Andrews on December 18, 1971, the flag on the clubhouse was lowered to half staff and all play on the course called on account of darkness.

# Whoo-Ha, Arnie!

### by Dan Jenkins

*Sometimes, even the best writers need to replace their divots. When Jenkins — novelist (Semi-Tough, Dead Solid Perfect), journalist, and nonpareil on the golf beat — realized the epic import of the final round of the 1960 U.S. Open, pride dictated that he retrace his steps.*

It was, I still believe, the most remarkable day in golf since Mary Queen of Scots found herself three down to an unbathed bagpiper and invented the back nine. And now, given all these years of reflection, it still seems as significant as the day Arnold Palmer first hitched up his trousers, the moment Jack Nicklaus decided to lose weight and fluff-dry his hair, and that interlude in the pro shop when Ben Hogan selected his first white cap.

Small wonder that every sportswriter present, including myself, choked at the typewriter. It was simply too big, too wildly exciting, too crazily suspenseful, too suffocatingly dramatic for any of us to do it justice.

What exactly happened? Oh, not much. Just a routine collision of three decades at one historical intersection.

On that afternoon, in the span of just eighteen holes, we witnessed the arrival of Nicklaus, the coronation of Palmer, and the end of Hogan. Nicklaus was a twenty-year-old amateur who would own the 1970s. Palmer was a thirty-year-old pro who would dominate the 1960s. Hogan was a forty-seven-year-old immortal who had overwhelmed the 1950s. While they had a fine supporting cast, it was primarily these three men who waged war for the U.S. Open championship on that Saturday of June 18, 1960. The battle was continuous, under a steaming Colorado sun at the Cherry Hills Country Club in Denver.

Things happened to them, around them.

Things happened in front of them, behind them.

Nobody knew where to go next, to see who had the lead, who was close, who had faltered.

Leaderboards changed faster than stoplights. And for a great while they were bleeding with red numbers.

In those days there was something known as Open Saturday. It is no longer part of golf — thanks to TV, no thanks, actually. But it was a day like no other; a day when the best golfers in the world were required to play thirty-six holes because it had always seemed to the USGA that a prolonged test of physical and mental stamina should go into the earning of the game's most important championship. Thus, Open Saturday lent itself to wondrous comebacks and funny collapses, and it provided a full day's ration of every emotion familiar to the athlete competing under pressure.

Open Saturday had been an institution with the USGA since its fourth championship in 1898, and there had been many a thriller before 1960, Saturdays that had tested the nerves and skill of the Bobby Joneses, the Gene Sarazens, the Walter Hagens, the Harry Vardons, the Byron Nelsons, the Sam Sneads, and, of course, the Ben Hogans.

But any serious scholar of the sport, or anyone fortunate enough to have been at Cherry Hills, is aware that the Open Saturday of Arnold, Jack, and Ben was extra special — a National Open that in meaning for the game continues to dwarf most of the others.

It was the Open in which Arnold Palmer shot a 65 in the last round and became the real Arnold Palmer. Threw his visor in the air, smoked a bunch of cigarettes, chipped in, drove a ball through a forest and onto a green, tucked in his shirttail, and lived happily ever after in the history books.

And that is pretty much what happened. But there is a constant truth about tournament golf: other men have to lose a championship before one man can win it. And never has the final eighteen of an Open produced as many losers as Cherry Hills did in 1960. When it was over, there were as many stretcher cases as there were shouts of "Whooha, go get 'em, Arnie." And that stood to reason after you considered that in those insane four hours Palmer came from seven strokes off the lead and from fifteenth place to grab a championship he had never even been in contention for.

Palmer had arrived in Denver as the favorite. Two months earlier he had taken his second Masters with what was beginning to be known to the wire services as a "charge." He had almost been confirmed as the Player of the New Era, though not quite. But as late as noon on Open Saturday, after three rounds of competition, you would hardly have heard his name mentioned in Denver. A list of the leaders through fifty-four holes shows how hopeless his position seemed. The scoreboard read:

| | | |
|---|---|---|
| Mike Souchak | 68 - 67 - 73 | — 208 |
| Julius Boros | 73 - 69 - 68 | — 210 |
| Dow Finsterwald | 71 - 69 - 70 | — 210 |
| Jerry Barber | 69 - 71 - 70 | — 210 |
| Ben Hogan | 75 - 67 - 69 | — 211 |
| Jack Nicklaus | 71 - 71 - 69 | — 211 |
| Jack Fleck | 70 - 70 - 72 | — 212 |
| Johnny Pott | 75 - 68 - 69 | — 212 |
| Don Cherry | 70 - 71 - 71 | — 212 |
| Gary Player | 70 - 72 - 71 | — 213 |
| Sam Snead | 72 - 69 - 73 | — 214 |
| Billy Casper | 71 - 70 - 73 | — 214 |
| Dutch Harrison | 74 - 70 - 70 | — 214 |
| Bob Shave | 72 - 71 - 71 | — 214 |
| Arnold Palmer | 72 - 71 - 72 | — 215 |

Through Thursday's opening round, Friday's second round, and right up until the last hole of the first eighteen on Saturday, this Open had belonged exclusively to Mike Souchak, a long-hitting, highly popular pro. His blazing total of 135 after thirty-six holes was an Open record. And as he stood on the eighteenth tee of Saturday's morning round, he needed only a par four for a 71 and a four-stroke lead on the field.

Then came an incident that gave everyone a foreboding about the afternoon. On Souchak's backswing, a camera clicked loudly. Souchak's drive soared out-of-bounds, and he took a double-bogey six for a 73. He never really recovered from the jolt. While the lead would remain his well into the afternoon, you could see Mike painfully allowing the tournament to slip away from him. He was headed for the slow death of a finishing 75 and another near miss, like the one he had suffered the previous year in the Open at Winged Foot up in Westchester County.

"A HUNK OF IRON PERFECT FOR ANY NUMBER OF HOUSEHOLD USES, SUCH AS POKING A FIRE OR KILLING A MOUSE, BUT SO PROGRAMMED THAT IT WILL HIT A GOLF BALL ONLY ON THE TOP HALF AND SEND IT CHATTERING, IN LINE-DRIVE CONFIGURATION, INTO THE NEAREST CLUMP OF IVY."

— JIM MURRAY, ON THE NINE-IRON

73

Much has been written about Arnold in the locker room at Cherry Hills between rounds on Open Saturday. It has become a part of golfing lore. As it happened, I was there, one of two people with Arnold. The other was Bob Drum, a writer then with the *Pittsburgh Press*. It was a position that allowed Drum to enjoy the same close relationship with Palmer that the *Atlanta Journal*'s O. B. Keeler once had with Bobby Jones.

Everybody had cheeseburgers and iced tea. We bathed our faces and arms with cold towels. It was too hot to believe that you could actually see snowcaps on the Rockies on the skyline.

As Palmer sat on the locker room bench, there was no talk at all of who might win, only of how short and inviting the course was playing, of how Mike Souchak, with the start he had, would probably shoot 269 if the tournament were a Pensacola Classic instead of the Open.

Arnold was cursing the first hole at Cherry Hills, a 346-yard par four with an elevated tee. Three times he had just missed driving the green. As he left the group to join Paul Harney for their 1:42 starting time on the final eighteen, the thing on his mind was trying to drive that first green. It would be his one Cherry Hills accomplishment.

"If I drive the green and get a birdie or an eagle, I might shoot 65," Palmer said. "What'll that do?"

Drum said, "Nothing. You're too far back."

"It would give me 280," Palmer said. "Doesn't 280 always win the Open?"

"Yeah, when Hogan shoots it," I said, laughing heartily at my own wit.

Arnold lingered at the doorway, looking at us as if he were waiting for a better exit line.

"Go on, boy," Drum said. "Get out of here. Go make your seven or eight birdies but shoot 73. I'll see you later."

Bob Drum had been writing Palmer stories since Palmer was the West Pennsylvania amateur champion. On a Fort Worth newspaper, I had been writing Ben Hogan stories for ten years, but I had also become a friend of Palmer's because I was a friend of Drum's.

Palmer left the room but we didn't, for the simple reason that Mike Souchak, the leader, would not be starting his last round for another fifteen or twenty minutes. But the fun began before that. It started for us when word drifted back to the locker room that Palmer had indeed driven the first green and two-putted for a birdie. He had not carried the ball 346 yards in the air, but he had nailed it good enough for it to burn a path through the high weeds the USGA had nurtured in front of the green to prevent just such a thing from happening. Palmer had in fact barely missed his eagle putt from twenty feet.

Frankly, we thought nothing of it. Nor did we think much of the news that Arnold had chipped in from thirty-five feet for a birdie at the second. What did get Bob Drum's attention was the distant thunder which signaled that Arnold had birdied the third hole. He had wedged to within a foot of the cup.

We were standing near the putting green by the clubhouse, and we had just decided to meander out toward Souchak when Drum said, "Care to join me at the fourth hole?"

We broke into a downhill canter.

As we arrived at the green, Palmer was in the process of drilling an eighteen-foot birdie putt into the cup. He was now four under through four, two under for the championship, only three strokes behind Souchak, and there were a lot of holes left to play.

We stooped under the ropes at the fifth tee, as our armbands entitled us to, and awaited Arnold's entrance. He came in hitching up the pants and gazed down the fairway. Spotting us, he strolled over.

"Fancy seeing you here," he said with a touch of slyness.

Then he drank the rest of my Coke, smoked one of my cigarettes, and failed to birdie the hole, a par five. On the other hand, he more than made up for it by sinking a curving twenty-five-footer for a birdie at the par-three sixth. At the seventh, he hit another splendid wedge to within six feet of the flag. He made the putt. And the cheers that followed told everybody on the golf course that Arnold Palmer had birdied six of the first seven holes.

It was history-book stuff. And yet for all those heroics it was absolutely unreal to look up at a scoreboard out on the course and learn that Arnold Palmer still wasn't leading the Open. Some kid named Jack Nicklaus was. That beefy guy from Columbus paired with Hogan, playing two groups ahead of Palmer. The amateur. Out in 32. Five under now for the tournament.

Bob Drum sized up the scoreboard for everyone around him.

"The fat kid's five under and the whole world's four under," he said.

That was true one minute and not true the next. By the whole world, Drum meant Palmer, Hogan, Souchak, Boros, Fleck, Finsterwald, Barber, Cherry, etc. It was roughly 3:30 then, and for the next half hour it was impossible to know who was actually leading, coming on, falling back, or what. Palmer further complicated things by taking a bogey at the eighth. He parred the ninth and was out in a stinging 30, five under on the round. But in harsh truth, as I suggested to Bob Drum at the time, he was still only three under for the tournament and two strokes off the pace of Nicklaus or Boros or Souchak — possibly all three. And God knows, I said, what Hogan, Fleck, and Cherry — not to mention Dutch Harrison, or even Ted Kroll — were doing while we were standing there talking.

Dutch Harrison, for example, had gone out very early and was working on a 69 and 283. And way back behind even Palmer was Ted Kroll, who had begun the round at 216, one stroke worse off than Palmer. Kroll and Jack Fleck had put almost the same kind of torch to Cherry Hills's front nine holes that Palmer had. Kroll had birdied five of the first seven holes, with one bogey included. Fleck had birdied five of the first six, also with a bogey included. Kroll was going to wind up firing the second-best round of the day, a 67, which would pull him into what later would look like a 200-way tie for third place at the popular figure of 283.

Meanwhile, we were out on the course thinking about Palmer's chances in all of this when Drum made his big pronouncement of the day.

"My man's knocked 'em all out," he said. "They just haven't felt the shock waves yet."

History has settled for Drum's analysis, and perhaps that is the truth of the matter after all. The story of the 1960 Open has been compressed into one sentence: Arnold Palmer birdied six of the first seven holes and won.

But condensations kill. What is missing is everything that happened after four o'clock. The part about Mike Souchak losing the lead for the first time only after he bogeyed the ninth hole. The part about Nicklaus blowing the lead he held all by himself when he took three ghastly putts from only ten feet at the thirteenth. This was the first real indication that they were all coming back to Palmer now, for Nicklaus's bogey dropped him into a four-way tie with Palmer, Boros, and Fleck.

But so much more is still missing from the condensation. Nicklaus's woeful inexperience as a young amateur cost him another three-putt bogey at the fourteenth hole, and so, as suddenly as he had grabbed the lead, he was out of it. Then it was around 4:45 and Palmer was sharing the lead with Hogan and Fleck, each of them four under. But like Nicklaus, Fleck would leave it on the greens. Boros had started leaving it on the greens and in the bunkers somewhat earlier. He was trapped at the fourteenth and eighteenth, for instance, and in between he blew a three-footer. In the midst of all this, Palmer was playing a steady back side of one birdie and eight pars on the way to completing his 65. And until the last two holes of the championship, the only man who had performed more steadily than Palmer, or seemed to be enduring the Open stress with as much steel as he, was — no surprise — Ben Hogan.

It was getting close to 5:30 when Hogan and Palmer were alone at four under par in the championship, and the two of them, along with everybody else — literally everyone on the golf course — had somehow wound up on the seventeenth hole, the seventy-first of the tournament.

The seventeenth at Cherry Hills is still a long, straightaway par five of 548 yards, with a green fronted by a pond. In 1960 it was a drive, a layup, and a pitch. And there they all were. Hogan and Nicklaus contemplating their pitch shots as the twosome of Boros and Player waited to hit their second shots, while the twosome of Palmer and Paul Harney stood back on the tee.

Hogan was faced with a delicate shot of about fifty yards to a pin sitting altogether too close to the water, on the front of the green, to try anything risky. Ben had hit thirty-four straight greens in regulation that Saturday. He needed only to finish with two pars for a 69 and a total of 280 — and nobody understood better than Hogan what it meant to reach the clubhouse first with a good score in a major.

Armed with all this knowledge, I knelt in the rough and watched Hogan address the shot and said brilliantly to Drum,

> "THE CHIP IS THE GREAT ECONOMIST OF GOLF."
> — BOBBY JONES

"He probably thinks he needs a birdie with Arnold behind him, but I'll guarantee you one thing — he'll be over the water."

At which point Hogan hit the ball in the water.

It was a foot shy of perfect, but it hit the bank and spun back in.

He made a bogey six. And in trying to erase that misfortune on the eighteenth with a huge drive, which might conceivably produce a birdie, he hooked his tee shot into the lake and suffered a triple-bogey seven. Sadly, only thirty minutes after he had been a co-leader with just two holes to go, Hogan finished in a tie for ninth place, four strokes away.

Second place then was left to the twenty-year-old with the crew cut, and Nicklaus's score of 282 remains the lowest total ever posted by an amateur in the Open. All in all, these were tremendous performances by an aging Hogan and a young Nicklaus. The two of them had come the closest to surviving Palmer's shock waves.

It was later on, back in the locker room, long after Palmer had slung his visor in the air for the photographers, that Ben Hogan said the truest thing of all about the day. Ben would know best.

He said, "I guess they'll say I lost it. Well, one more foot and the wedge on seventeen would have been perfect. But I'll tell you something. I played thirty-six holes today with a kid who should have won this Open by ten shots."

Jack Nicklaus would start winning Opens and other major titles soon enough as a pro, of course. But wasn't it nice to have Arnold around first?

# In Conversation with Ben Crenshaw

*One of golf's true renaissance men, Ben Crenshaw is more than just a two-time Masters champion and victorious Ryder Cup captain; he is also a passionate student, graceful essayist, and one of the most respected of the new breed of course designers. It seemed only natural that when a treasure trove of long-forgotten photographs of Bobby Jones's swing and the Master's handwritten notes on golf's fundamentals was found, Crenshaw would be asked to help give it shape for today's golfer. The resulting book, 1998's* Classic Instruction, *is something of a collaboration across time between two remarkable sportsmen, and as good a hook as any to invite one master of the game to talk about another.*

JS: When you first saw Jones's notes and photos you must have felt like you'd gone back in time.

BC: To see these photographs jump out at you, and to actually see his pencil in yellow legal hand, his thoughts coming to fruition, I mean it was like viewing a piece of history. And he wrote about the game so beautifully. Some of his writings about golf are, I think, part of why golf is popular today.

JS: Using your golfer's eye, what do you see in his swing?

BC: Number one, the implements he played with. The hickory shafts promoted a little bit more of a "hand-y" style. There was more footwork involved then. There was more of a body turn, more of a freer hip turn, and shoulder turn. Today, players are taught to keep their feet a little more flat on the ground; not so much footwork, but still to have a very full shoulder turn. His swing is well rounded, but maybe a little bit on the flatter side. There was a flatter plane, because he always said that he wanted to keep the ball down, out of the breeze a little bit, and he wanted a running ball.

JS: What about his chipping and pitching? He didn't have all the utility clubs we have now.

BC: No he didn't. He had to be a little more artful, because he played the shots with probably a little straighter-faced club, meaning that no one tried to loft the ball unless they absolutely had to in those days. You kept the ball on the ground because that was the safer method. It was a very, very delicate proposition when you played the shorter club.

JS: What do you see in his putting?

BC: He stood with his feet close together, and he wanted to make sure that his putter swung. That meant taking it back a long way and bringing it smooth. He wanted to let the ball sort of get in the way of his stroke, meaning that he thought the longer you take the club back, the less that you had to hit the ball at impact. He said it's perfectly okay for your knees and body to get involved, even in the little stroke!

JS: If you could give Bobby Jones a modern set of clubs and put him out on the golf course, how do you think he would do?

BC: I have no doubt that Bob Jones would have won in any era. There was just such a touch of genius about him.

JS: It's funny, but if you look at movies of golfers from the '20s, the swing looks so different from today's, yet Jones's actually looks almost contemporary. Do you think he was a transition between the older and more modern eras?

BC: Probably so. I would say that he was maybe the start of a transition. His turn was almost like Sam Snead's; they both had a beautiful, beautiful big shoulder turn. Byron Nelson really is sort of credited with bringing the swing into the modern era, because he and Ben Hogan were among the first players who really started excelling with the steel shaft. Remember, steel shafts do a lot of the work for you now. You had to be very precise in the era of hickory shafts. You had to hit the ball very solidly. There was not that much margin of error built into those clubs.

> "I PITCH THE BALL WHENEVER POSSIBLE BECAUSE THERE ARE NO HAZARDS IN THE AIR."
> — BYRON NELSON

JS: Had you met Jones, what would you have said to him?

BC: Very simply, I would have just loved to shake his hand and say what a pleasure it is for golfers to have what you have left us.

JS: Jones himself was a fine writer on the game. What is it about golf that's led to so much fine writing?

BC: Well, golf has been around for 500 years, and it has attracted all sorts of literary and talented people who feel passionate about the sport, and they want to relate it because it makes deep impressions on them. The bottom line in golf is that the human foibles that we all go through when playing the game are really no different than those of the previous century — or earlier. The implements have changed, but the thoughts still remain.

It's the most elusive game! This stationary object that sits there and dares you to do certain things. And you can do wonderful things and magical things, but you can do diabolical things, as well.

JS: I can certainly vouch for the diabolical ones.

BC: Me, too.

# The King and His Plaque

There are many monuments throughout the golfing world to the immense achievement of Arnold Palmer, but none is as inspirational to the common duffer as the marker beside the eighteenth tee at Rancho Park Golf Course in Los Angeles. It reminds us that golfing misery is not personal; it's shared by all.

In the 1961 L.A. Open, Palmer stepped up needing only a par five to card a second-round 69. He hit a good drive, but pushed his three-wood out-of-bounds onto the driving range to the right. He tried his three-wood again, and again, out-of-bounds to the right. Sticking with the three, Palmer hooked his next shot onto the street left of the course. Not willing to give up, he hooked another out-of-bounds. Five strokes, four penalties.

Lieing nine in precisely the same spot he had been lieing one, Palmer again ripped a his three-wood. He landed that one on the green, and ultimately carded a septuple bogey on the hole. When asked how he could possibly take a twelve, The King replied royally, "I missed the putt for the eleven."

—J. S.

# Watching Hogan Practice

### by Pat Ward-Thomas

*Ward-Thomas (1913-1982) was the* Guardian's *eminent golf correspondent for nearly three decades. His love of the game was a truly epic affair: as an RAF pilot in World War II, he was captured by the Germans and interned in a POW camp, where he wound up building a rough nine-hole course. He and his fellow prisoners regularly played with clubs and balls provided by the Red Cross until the Russian advance from the east helped free them.*

Often at the Masters we would watch Hogan practice.… I would sit on the grass by his bag and watch the shots stream into the morning sunshine. On one occasion Hogan was alone on the practice ground and was disposed to chat at intervals in the hitting of shots. Most of these had been straight or fractionally right-to-left, and I asked him to fade one. Without any apparent alteration in stance or angle of club face, a three-iron shot rifled away. For an instant it seemed that the ball would not fade, but as it reached the peak of its flight it leaked slightly to the right, only a few feet from the original line.

When I asked how this was done and what was in his mind, Hogan looked straight at me and said, "You are too old;" there was a pause and he added, "So am I; it would take too long to explain." I think he meant that he shaped his shots by feel rather than by any physical adjustment. This was fascinating, for he had brought the science of hitting a golf ball nearer to mechanical precision than anyone had, and yet the abstract quality of feel still played an important part.

Hogan's manner could be disturbingly direct, especially to those whom he thought were seeking a cheap story or quote. It was said that he could express more in fewer words than anyone. If a monosyllable sufficed, he would not embellish it. But once he knew a writer was sincerely interested, he was polite and patient and would give his full attention to the subject. There was nothing of hypocrisy or false modesty about him, nothing superficial in a land where the superficial abounds. The intensity of his quest for perfection in golf can rarely, if ever, have been matched, and it was a lonely pursuit. As he said that day, "I must be alone, way to hell out there by myself, I just love it." He seemed to have no need of people, of cheering crowds, finding complete fulfillment in hitting perfect golf shots. There is no way of disproving his assertion that "I know that I have had greater satisfaction than anyone who ever lived out of the hitting of golf shots," but he must have been very close to the mark.

# On Golf, Baseball, DiMaggio and Williams

### *by Sam Snead*

*Golf's most beautiful swing? It's hard disputing that it belongs to the garrulous Slammin' Sammy, who used it to win seven majors and eighty-one PGA tournaments overall, playing both his fair balls and the ones he hit foul.*

Baseball was one of my first loves and a sport I still enjoy today. I was a very good player, I think, and a good student of the game. I was a pitcher, a pretty good one, and I even toured around playing semi-pro ball. I applied my baseball experiences wherever I could to help me out of the fixes I got myself into in golf.

I played golf with many of the best baseball players in the history of the game. Some of them could really hold their own on the golf course. Ted Williams, Joe DiMaggio, Yogi Berra, and Mickey Mantle were among my favorites.... DiMaggio had the most talent for golf, but I don't think he played or practiced much. He carried a nine handicap and could shoot 73 in a pro-am. Jimmy Demaret and I told him he could be a scratch player if he wanted. He said, "No, I'll just take my nine." And then he won almost everything he played in....

Ted Williams and I were friends and spent many a day involved in our favorite other sport: fishing.... Williams did an analysis of my baseball swing for *Golf Digest* back in 1960. It was good fun. We always had a friendly rivalry going about something, whether it was hitting a baseball, hitting a golf ball, or fishing.

I analyzed his golf swing in the same article and said that Ted might have been the first southpaw golf champion. He had that delayed-hit action, holding his wrists back until the last second. But Ted was also a stubborn pull hitter in baseball (remember the famous "Williams Shift"?) and would have been a hooker in golf. He concentrated well, crowds didn't bother him, and he had a good touch, which I discovered watching him land large fish like tarpon on light lines.

We used to argue about which hand provided the power in the swing. I felt it was the left because you can pull more than you can push — you pull with the left hand in baseball or golf if you are right-handed. We argued about which sport was more difficult. The way Ted told it, baseball is harder because you have a man throwing a ball ninety miles an hour — and sometimes it's ducking away from you. Williams always thought golfers were soft — nobody said "boo" on the golf course. The ball was just sitting there waiting for you to hit it. I'm sure he thought he was right.

I told him golf was harder because we've got to play all our foul balls. And you have no teammates to help you fit that little ball into a four-and-a-quarter-inch hole.

# What Spooks the Bear

*Part of mastering course management is understanding that a) no golfer is bulletproof and b) every shot has an element of risk. Early in his career, Jack Nicklaus, as mentally tough as any golfer ever, admitted he had on-course fears and then systematically confronted them. Assessing the shot results he considered most painful, Nicklaus identified — from harshest to least punitive — the sufferings he accepted were there but would personally prefer to avoid.*

1. Out-of-bounds
2. Lost ball
3. Unplayable lie
4. Water
5. Woods
6. Severe rough
7. Deep or severely lipped bunkers
8. Steeply angled lie
9. Shallow bunker
10. Light rough
11. Slightly angled lie

Naturally, if even the slightest mistake in shot-making could result in either of the first two on his list, Nicklaus would never even consider it. Would you? If the answer's "yes," you probably won't win eighteen Majors.    —J. S.

# 6
# THE FAIRWAYEST OF
# THEM ALL

(WOMEN AND GOLF)

# A Woman's Handicap Begins Off-Course

### *by Glenna Collett Vare*

*Dubbed "the female Bobby Jones," Hall-of-Famer Glenna Collett Vare (1903-1989) won a record six U.S. Women's Amateur titles, and once strung together an unimaginable sixteen tournament victories in a row. Her name is inscribed on the trophy given annually by the LPGA to the golfer with the lowest scoring average. Her exuberance, personality, and style are inscribed on every page of her 1929 memoir,* Ladies in the Rough, *from which this is taken. The first important golf book written by a woman, it was part memoir and part instruction, quite smart, often funny, sweetly acerbic, and in the final wish in this excerpt, heartbreakingly poignant. It is the golfing equivalent of the observation that Ginger Rogers could do everything Fred Astaire did — only backwards and in high heels.*

Sometimes I wish I were a man. There would be so much more fun in golf — and so many fewer strokes. After all, the most satisfying rounds, although not always the most enjoyable, are those that cost the fewest strokes. At least, that is true when you have become golf-conscious and are striving for par figures....

The margin between the sexes on the links is not wholly one of muscle.... There is the matter of costume, for one thing. This may not impress the male golfer as being of great moment, but I assure you that it is.... Clothes do not make the golfer; that is, if you limit the statement to men golfers.

A woman cares as much about her appearance as she does about her score. And, from a purely technical standpoint, the best-looking costume is not always the most helpful; nor is the "sensible" costume most becoming. The wide-hemmed skirts that permit the attitudes necessary in striving for a 200-yard drive or chipping from the face of the bunker do not hang gracefully on the feminine form.

Frankly, they are dangerously close to dowdiness, and it is a tribute to woman's passionate devotion to golf that she will wear this "sensible" skirt, knowing that, while it adds yards to her drives, it detracts much from her charm....

The plus fours of the male are an ideal costume. Feminine ingenuity has devised no costume so perfect for golf. Some women have worn them in tournaments. There is much to be said for knickers. All that can be said against them is that the average woman does not look well in them, and well she knows it. Their undoubted utility can never outweigh their obvious futility as a means of adornment.

Such is the decision of thousands of women golfers. And that is that, for golf is not everything. If men could play golf more efficiently in skirts, we might confidently expect to see them so garb themselves; but the ladies, unfortunately for their golfing reputations, will not wear plus fours. And it is probably just as well, for the resulting snickers at the women in knickers would so disconcert them that they would lose whatever gain in athletic efficiency the innovation would bring.

* * *

Feminine golf carries another handicap that is not so marked in the men's ranks. A woman is easily flustered by a variety of little things to which she should give no notice. Psychologists undoubtedly can give adequate reasons for the lady golfer's jumpy nerves; we know it as "tournament nervousness." It explains why so many women score a thirty-seven on one round and a forty-seven on the next.

When a man plays golf, he can forget everything except the business in hand. He lays aside his business problems and steels himself with concentration. He remembers only to keep his head down and his eye on the ball. He resolutely puts out of his mind everything that could possibly add to his score.

A woman has no such capacity for concentration. A golf professional once told me that was his most aggravating problem — to teach his fair duffers to concentrate. In the midst of a match the woman golfer will think of and dwell on many things that have not the slightest bearing on the game. Did she order the roast for dinner? Heavens, no! And there

> "I JUST LOOSEN MY GIRDLE AND LET THE BALL HAVE IT."
> — BABE DIDRICKSON

goes a slice. Why did she invite the Browns for Friday, when the cook is off? In contemplation of that situation she tops her mashie.

In the midst of the serious business of lining up the putt, if her tortured mind permits her at length to reach the green, she suddenly remembers that Junior went to school that morning without a handkerchief. So the putt runs past the cup, and coming back, she is short.

A man would consider such things trifles of no importance, or else easily remedied. But a woman cannot forget trifles. Her life is made up of trifles. She must give thought to other matters even when she is playing golf, else her score as a wife would not break a hundred.

\* \* \*

*[But even if an exemplary woman golfer had a man's strength, wardrobe and determination, she'd still be playing with disadvantages.]*
… She approaches the first tee with the male champion, her mind on the golf match and nothing else. He winds up

"THE POINT IS THAT IT DOESN'T MATTER IF YOU LOOK LIKE A BEAST BEFORE OR AFTER YOU HIT, AS LONG AS YOU LOOK LIKE A BEAUTY AT THE MOMENT OF IMPACT."
— SEVE BALLESTEROS

vigorously and gives the ball a ride. The hypothetical lady prepares to drive — and another innate feminine weakness is disclosed. She wonders if she presents a graceful appearance, decides that she might end up in some awkward posture if she, too, attempted to give the ball a ride. So she shortens her swing, sacrificing distance to decorum.

A man does not care whether he is awkward-looking. A long tee shot soothes any hurt to his pride. But a woman, unfortunately, cannot so forget herself. She has a duty more important than golf — the age-old feminine duty never to look ridiculous if she can help it.

With the last putt sinking into the eighteenth cup, the men are prepared for their round the next day. But the ladies, because complexion is more important to most than par golf, must first retire to their boudoirs and apply cold creams and lotions.

These are some of the reasons why a woman cannot compete on even terms with a man at golf, even supposing she is his equal in strength and skill. The handicaps for the ordinary woman are still more numerous.

She does not have nearly so many opportunities to play.

The busy broker can slam his desk shut at three o'clock, call a crony, and drive to the links, where they quiet their consciences by pretending to discuss business affairs. In fact, it is a male proverb that many big deals are made on the golf-links.

Women have not yet figured out a method of running the household from the links. You cannot well take the cook and maid and children's nurse with you for a foursome — deciding the menu on the first green, planning the spring house-cleaning as you proceed along the fairway of the 500-yard dogleg hole, and deciding Junior's program while blasting out of a trap.

If a husband is late for dinner, he passes it off lightly by blaming the fussy foursome ahead; but imagine the dialogue that would follow a wife's attempt to offer the same explanation for a late dinner! I do not contend that these matters should not be as they are. Still, they do make it difficult at times for a woman to give proper attention to her game.

The etiquette of golf calls for certain formulas that are not found in any book of instructions. There is one expletive for a topped drive; milder ones for hooks and slices. For putts that rim the cup there are several recognized expletives. Also, it is part of the ritual that the caddie, the greens committee, the gallery, or your opponent can be held responsible for any lack of perfection in your play. That is to say, these things are permissible if you are a man. And undoubtedly they are an aid in keeping down blood pressure. But the most that is allowed women is an apologetic, half-swallowed "Damn" under the most trying circumstances. Women, gentle creatures, are not expected to utter harsh oaths, and that is too bad. There are probably occasions when oaths are helpful if not proper.

George Bernard Shaw has a naive theory that women are only human beings who, by force of habit and convention, wear skirts instead of trousers. He is not in favor of coddling them. The American golfing male dissents. He is chivalrous — would not have her dainty ears shocked by man's robust golfing conversation. He guards her by telling her to stay off the links....

I do not wish I were a man except sometimes, when my drives only come within a full shot of my opponent's. I envy him his spirit of freedom, his independence of trifles, his disdain of convention, his disregard of appearances, and his childlike conviction, if he is a golfer, that golf is the most important thing on this bunkered sphere.

# A Course of Their Own

## by Marcia Chambers

*Former* New York Times *reporter Chambers exposed the enormity of golf's grass ceiling in her powerful 1995 chronicle,* The Unplayable Lie: The Untold Story of Women and Discrimination in American Golf. *In it, she tells the story of a visionary when she sets out to explore whether women, like men, might have a course of their own.*

. . . They might and they did. The founder of the first women's club of the 20th century was Marion Hollins. She was not only a ranking golfer, having won the women's national championship in 1921; she was also a champion horsewoman and, most important of all, an influential socialite who could assemble powerful and well-placed women. She called her club the Women's National Golf and Tennis Club, on Long Island.... The need for a women's club had become apparent after a num-

> "WHY AM I USING A NEW PUTTER? BECAUSE THE OLD ONE DIDN'T FLOAT TOO WELL."
> — CRAIG STADLER AT THE 1993 U.S. OPEN

ber of new clubs opened on Long Island and women were told they would not be allowed to play on weekends and holidays....

Marion Hollins's dream was to bring out the best in women's golf, and to do that, she felt, women had to have a course of their own, one that would test women without sacrificing length or hazards. Before the course opened on Memorial Day 1924, Miss Hollins had attracted some 400 members, many prominent socially and in the world of golf and tennis.... Members paid $1,000 a share with annual dues of $150.... Many of the women came from the metropolitan New York area, but the roster also included women from San Francisco and other major cities in the United States....

Women's National was a course designed for the great women amateurs of the day. Miss Hollins visited England and Scotland and studied golf courses there. Architect Devereux Emmet designed a course that was not excessively long yet challenged the women with clever placement of hazards....

The Women's National Golf and Tennis Club lasted a relatively short seventeen years. Like many clubs of the day, it didn't survive the Depression. But Marion Hollins had not been an active force in the club's later years, for she had moved her home and her allegiance to the Monterey Bay in California, where she discovered and built (with the famed architect Alister MacKenzie) a great golf course and real-estate development at Pasatiempo. She struck it rich in oil, and her profits fueled the Pasatiempo estates through the Depression years, when it thrived as a social and golfing mecca with the continuing infusion of her money.

But by 1938 Pasatiempo Estates Development was in deep financial trouble and Miss Hollins was forced to sell. Two years later she severed all connections with the place. She had lost her entire fortune in just ten years and died, four years later, in nearby Pacific Grove … at the age of fifty-one. Pasatiempo remains as a ranking course, open to the public, and a testament to Marion Hollins's vision.

# Tee for Two Genders

### by Amy Bennet Pascoe

*What is truly remarkable about this 1899 examination of women golfers is not the reach of its geography, its claim for the game's origins, its shifts in tone, or how much the theoretical threesome it identifies can be found on either side of the gender line. No. It's the revelation that once upon a time a round could actually be completed in two hours.*

The lady golfer is a distinct genus, belonging to the order of Amazona, or athletic women. Interesting and instructive are the characteristics of the species — pity space prohibits a detailed account of its acquired and inherited habits; they are, however, very obvious to the eruditi in girls' games and sports. Lady golfers are found at every age, in all parts of the world. With curls down their backs, in abbreviated skirts, we meet them flying over the Shinnecock Hills, U.S.A., or silver-haired, bespectacled, bonneted, they waggle on the Wimbledon Common!

Amid the desert near Baghdad they hole out, win championships in New Zealand, and tea at the neat chalet pavilion on the top of the Mustapha slopes, Algiers. Their chief habitat is the United Kingdom; here they possess over 120 clubs, of which nearly all have been instituted since the eighties. The evolution of the lady player may be studied by those who have no acquaintance with fossils or comparative anatomy. We trace her descent through Mary Queen of Scots to the fishwives of Musselburgh. On the principle that a Norman ancestor is more usually quoted than a Victorian greengrocer grandmamma, the fact of Mary having played in the fields round Seton is better known than the instance of the fish ladies' competition in 1810 for a new Barcelona handkerchief, a new creel, and shawl. Although we cannot determine the exact sequence of women drivers and putters who preceded Queen Mary into the remotest hazards of history, we have those records of their near relative — the male player — which guide us in the right direction; for it would not be possible that Scotch father, brother, and husband should play the game during many hundred years without their womenfolk joining in foursomes, or engaging among themselves in terrible single combat. Indeed, it may be proved that the discovery of golf was due to a woman. The prehistoric shepherd who hit a pebble with his crook into a neighboring rabbit hole, and thus accidentally originated the game, did so in a fit of ill-humor that his shepherdess was late for the rendezvous!

The reason of woman's tardy introduction on Southron greens is that her presence there was somewhat severely interdicted in the Badminton (Library) book: firstly, lest men should find it hard to decide between flirting and playing the game; secondly, because of the volubility of female tongue and skirt; and thirdly, should she volunteer to score there could be no manner of doubt in whose favor she would do so! However, as women grew more independent in their habits, cultivated a love of fresh air and sport, lady golfers became naturalized in England, and notwithstanding a length of prize list and a shortness of course, factors not favorable to the production of first-class play, attention to style, keenness, and practice have developed within the last five years a game which elicits high praise in all parts where their championship has been held. Critical, able judges pronounce the drive of our best players to be both long and straight, approach a matter of surprise, their putting more cool and accurate than men's.

Lady golfers may be classed under three heads, and treated of individually, viz.: the Golfer, scratch or handicap, the Pot Hunter, the Player.

The Golfer is often one of the younger and latest members of the club. A good match and a good score are her pleasures. She takes a genuine interest in links and clubs. From her the secretary hears no complaints of the difficulties on the course or the unfairness of her luck. She is a favorite with the handicap committee, because a reduction of her odds is followed by no outcry; it dares curtail her allowance on any improvement of form shown, not waiting for a win; her ambition being a championship, not a buttonhook!

"YOU'RE ONLY HERE FOR A SHORT VISIT. DON'T HURRY. DON'T WORRY. AND BE SURE TO SMELL THE FLOWERS ALONG THE WAY."
— WALTER HAGEN

The Pot Hunter — these professional prize-catchers are fortunately not common, but most of us have had the opportunity of studying their habits. Their only enjoyment is in winning. They are no sportswomen. If they lose, we know that we shall all hear about their bad luck. The way that bad luck "goes" for them is extraordinary. According to them, lies are infinitely worse in the particular spot where their ball rests than anywhere else on the links, even in the bunkers! The hazards seem to get up and follow them round the course! They have never been properly handicapped, yet most of them have played a long time and belong to many clubs. The fashion of undervaluing one's own powers, especially when accompanied by an overappreciation of those of others, is so unusual in life that when we find it on the links we may confidently assert that such modesty is incompatible with morality. Pot Hunters never seem to have any game of their own to think about, but they make up for this by taking a 500 horsepower interest in other people's.

The Player — happy, lighthearted, irresponsible players!

All serious golfers love you. Sparkling, gaseous, bright, an effervescence of youth and amusement. We recognize you by your fluttering pretty dress, merry laughter, irrelevant movements. You hurry out to the tee, and rush back again for balls! You putt and talk with the flag in the hole; and add up the score on the green while cracks wait to play their approach. Such incidents as stymies, honors, strokes, you take no note of. When after a round, where we have seen you and caddies walking off instead of on the course, with a handsome allowance of twenty-four you win an enameled brooch, we are pleased and congratulate you. We do not even expostulate when, on the point of striking off the tee, we are suddenly startled and miss the globe by hearing eager voices discuss Mrs B.'s last dance from an adjacent green. No! We glance at the bright young faces so unconscious of enormity of that offense which has cost us our record round, and — forgive. Healing influence of youth and good spirits! Desert not our links for the lawn-tennis courts and hockey fields. To preserve you we will cede the golfers' unwritten rule of silence. Talk on, therefore, unrebuked. For you are always talking as fast as you can. Casual observers might think you had nothing to do with the game, and had merely come out for two hours' hard conversational exercise! Nevertheless we like you. You are not always in trouble, neither do you worry about other people's handicaps.

# 7
# READING THE GREEN

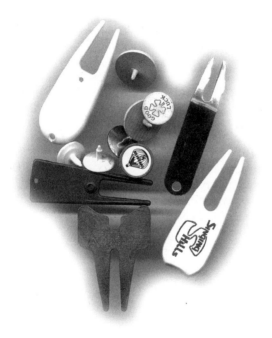

(COURSE DESIGN)

# The Course Beautiful

### by A. W. Tillinghast

*Philadelphia-born Alfred Warren Tillinghast (1874-1942) learned both how to play golf and how to design golf courses from the Scottish master himself — Old Tom Morris. A scratch handicapper and able writer as well as an editor at* Golf Illustrated *magazine while establishing his architectural chops, Tillinghast left a long paper trail of his thoughts about what makes a good golf course. Only a fool might argue that the creator of Baltusrol G.C., Winged Foot G. C., Quaker Ridge G. C., Bethpage State Park, and Philadelphia Cricket Club and the redesigner of Newport Country Club failed to practice what he preached.*

It seems to me that he who plans any hole for golf should have two aims: first, to produce something which will provide a true test of the game, and then to consider every conceivable way to make it as beautiful as possible. He should have in mind not only the skill and brawn of golfers but their eyes as well....

Certainly the playing qualities of any hole must be the first consideration, and there can be no comparison between the work of one who has adhered solely to it and that of the master of landscaping, who possesses a general idea of the requirements of modern golf. There are many truly picturesque courses which are otherwise undistinguished, and there are fine tests of golf as devoid of beauty as Mary Ellen's calico. Any real player would not speak of them in the same breath. But is it not a fact that the great courses, those that are talked of most, combine both qualities?

It is likely that fully 75 percent of golfers are keenly appreciative of the striking beauty of a picturesque hole. This estimate is conservative. But there are others who do not care a rap about their surroundings, so absorbed are they in hard play. I recall an incident of many years ago when a four-ball match came to a teeing ground which afforded a particularly impressive view of marsh-meadow stretching away to beach and ocean. One of the players spoke of it, but his partner exclaimed: "To hell with the view; we're two down!" I wonder which was the happier in his golf?

I believe that there are a goodly number of players who find their golf a mighty good excuse to get close to nature. There are thousands of businessmen closing their office desks every day and turning expectantly to the links, expecting what? The breaking of a hundred? Not much! That rare feat might happen to their extreme satisfaction. It might, but the one thing which everyone is sure of is a glorious afternoon in the open with

> "THE HARDEST SHOT IS A MASHIE AT NINETY YARDS FROM THE GREEN, WHERE THE BALL HAS TO BE PLAYED AGAINST AN OAK TREE, BOUNCED BACK INTO A SAND TRAP, HITS A STONE, BOUNCES ON THE GREEN AND THEN ROLLS INTO THE CUP. THAT SHOT IS SO DIFFICULT I HAVE MADE IT ONLY ONCE."
>
> — ZEPPO MARX

songs of birds in his ears rather than constantly tinkling bells and jangling noises; with the four walls of a room replaced by a delightful, ever-changing sight of meadow and trees and brooks, or broad stretches of ocean sands and water....

Fortunately our modern constructors are leaning very heavily on Nature. Every artificial formation today is made to appear as pleasing to the eye as possible. Formal mounds are giving way to creations which do not clash with their surroundings. Teeing grounds are taking on the contours of surroundings to a great extent, instead of the pawky little terraced, boxlike pulpits which seemed to shriek of wheelbarrows and spades. Instead of plunging headlong through a grove, felling and uprooting ruthlessly, some respect is being paid to fine old trees which stand out gloriously as "small-stuff" has been removed and the fairway gracefully sweeps around in dogleg and elbow.

I have in mind a line from a bit of verse, I think written by the late Joyce Kilmer — "But only God can make a tree." And

I think there is nothing more beautiful to look upon than a fine tree. Yet how many great specimens have been destroyed by the builders of golf courses, who had no eye for the beautiful nor ingenuity enough to find a way to let them stand, not only to add charm to courses but actually to help the play.

I plead guilty to the removal of many trees, but never have I given instructions for the destruction of a fine one without genuine regret, and then only when it was imperative. We may play around trees but certainly the only route to a hole must never be over or through them. Then, too, we must not have them directly by our putting greens, for their branches deflect many erring shots to fortunate finishes....

Some streams are unsightly when they might be made picturesque with little expense and thought. And so with many other features. On one course there stood a ruin, and the committee intended to raze it. They were persuaded to make a feature of it and with practically no cost it was made notable.

But let it be understood that I do not advocate the beautifying of the course at the expense of its playing qualities....

The course beautiful adds much to the pleasure of golf without detracting in the least from its qualities as a test. Even those players who are not analytical will have strong inclinations to certain courses over others. Aside from the fact that they probably fancy the places where they have scored best, the chances are that subconsciously they have admired the scenery a bit....

# Left-Handed Golf Courses

### *by Rube Goldberg*

*The celebrated left hand of cartoonist Reuben Lucius Goldberg (1883-1970) was best known for its skills at engineering amazingly complex and hilariously funny contraptions for performing the simplest and most mundane jobs. But there was a serious side to Goldberg, too.*

## The Inventions of Professor Lucifer G. Butts, A

PROFESSOR BUTTS' LANDLADY HITS HIM OVER THE HEAD WITH A PITCHER FOR NONPAYMENT OF RENT AND HE DISCOVERS A SURE WAY TO KEEP THE HEAD DOWN DURING A GOLF SHOT. GOLFER(A) SWINGS CLUB(B) AND HITS BRANCH OF TREE(C) SHAKING APPLES DOWN ON KETTLE-DRUM(D). CADDIE(E) HEARING NOISE THINKS A THUNDER STORM IS APPROACHING AND RUNS FOR CLUB HOUSE, STUMBLING OVER GOLF BAG(F) AND PUSHING FLAG POLE(G) AGAINST BAG OF PEANUTS(H) WHICH BREAKS AND THROWS PEANUTS IN BASKET(I). AS SQUIRREL(J) JUMPS INTO BASKET TO GET THE PEANUTS, HIS WEIGHT RAISES END OF PADDLE(K) AND DRAWS FISH(L) OUT OF WATER HAZARD. HUNGRY SEAL(M) SEEING FISH FLAPS HIS FLIPPERS(N) FOR JOY AND CAUSES BREEZE TO ENTER FUNNEL(O) THEREBY BLOWING MARDI-GRAS TICKLER(P) WHICH STRAIGHTENS OUT AND DEPOSITS DOLLAR BILL(Q) NEXT TO GOLF BALL, FOCUSSING EYES OF PLAYER ON THE SPOT DURING SWING.
IF YOU MISS THE BALL AND SWING INTO APPLE TREE OFTEN ENOUGH YOU CAN HAVE APPLE SAUCE FOR DINNER.

*He won the 1948 Pulitzer Prize for his editorial cartoons in the* New York Sun. *He was also quite serious about his golf, though you'd never know it from the left-handed observations that follow, concocted in 1924 for* The American Golfer.

I have been trying to play golf for the last seven years and have been reading about the game for twice as long. I get no comfort out of the continuous flow of golf reform literature that bellows and splashes against the shores of duffer island. Those who are suggesting new improvements are tackling the game from the wrong end.

By RUBE GOLDBERG

When I read that the new rules prohibit the use of corrugated club ends it has as much effect on me as if I had just heard that the Gaekwar of Baroda had issued a decree calling for purple tassels on all elephant saddles on Mondays and Fridays. The only good my backspin mashie ever did me was to use it as an onion grater when we were fortunate enough to have caviar sandwiches on picnics. Some people think the new metal shafts are a great improvement over the old wood-

> "THE GREATEST COMPLIMENT THAT CAN BE PAID TO THE ARCHITECT IS FOR PLAYERS TO THINK THAT HIS ARTIFICIAL WORK IS NATURAL."
> — ALISTAIR MACKENZIE

en ones. I have tried both and I would do just as well with rhubarb or asparagus. Every time they bring out a new ball called "The Purple Flash" or "The Comet's Tail" or "The Galloping Dandruff" I laugh so loud I wake up my caddie. I made the best drive of my whole golfing career with a meatball I had picked up by mistake from a passing lunch wagon.

Another thing that seems to take up a lot of time and energy among those who are sincerely but unwisely seeking new antidotes for the duffer's poisonous mistakes is wearing apparel. I have actually gone out on the links carrying eighteen sweaters — one for every hole. Each one of the sweaters, according to the ad, was built to give the player a particular advantage in playing certain shots. Some were fashioned to keep the neck rigid, others were made to keep the elbows dry when playing chip shots out of the ocean, and still others were designed with special cartridge belts for carrying spare pencils with which to write down extra large scores. The sweaters were all different, but my shots all remained the same.

I even went and purchased a pair of those terrible-looking English knickers that are baggy enough to hold a radio set, and stop somewhere between the knee and the ankle. They don't look like short pants and they don't look like long pants. They are a first cousin to balloon tires but don't give you near the mileage. I played one round in the pair that I bought and my caddie said to me just before he left, "Gee, your old man must be a pretty big guy, if you can wear his pants cut down and they're still too big for you." I gave the pants to my wife's sister who was having a garden party at her place in the country. She used them for Chinese lanterns.

As I said before, the reformers are trying to reform the game from the wrong end. The thing that needs changing is not the golf ball or the golf club or the golf trousers. It is the golf course. I am surprised that nobody has ever thought of suggesting the left-handed golf course. The left-handed golf course is bound to come if the game is to survive. It is an absolute necessity — for me at least.

I forgot to mention that I am left-handed — and there must be thousands of other unfortunates in this country like myself. I have been advised to switch to right-handed. But why should I? I have been eating soup for forty years with my left hand and I am not boasting when I say that my shirt front is as clean as the average man's. In the ordinary course of things it is no handicap to be left-handed. No woman ever refused to bow to me when I tipped my hat with my left hand — that is, no woman who knew me. I never made a waiter sore by handing him a tip with my left hand.

When I take a practice swing at home people look in through the window and say, "Good morning, Mister Sarazen." But when I go out on the golf course and take the same identical swing, the ball doesn't seem to go anywhere. So I know it must be the fault of the course. Logic is logic.

Here are a few of the handicaps I suffer when I play on the regulation course: when the average player shoots, he stands facing the other people on the tee. Being left-handed I must stand with my back to the crowd. Besides wondering whether or not they are giving me the raspberry, I must try to be a gentleman and say each time I step up to the ball, "Excuse my back." And you know that any talk during a shot throws a man off his stance — even if it be his own voice.

In standard golf courses most of the out-of-bounds limits are on the left side of the fairway. A sliced shot always puts me out-of-bounds. So I naturally stand well around to the right on every tee to play safe, so my drive will slice back into the fairway. Then for some reason or other I don't slice at all. My shot goes straight and I hit the president of the club, who is playing three fairways to the right. This puts me in continual bad standing, besides giving all the club members the extra trouble of finding a new president.

Another thing. When I make a beautiful shot right on the green next to the pin I invariably find that I have played for the wrong green. My left-handed vision has given me a cockeyed idea of the course.

My greatest handicap is in the traps, where I must admit I spend a good part of my weekends. It takes an experienced miner to go down into a hole with nothing but the blue sky as his only area of vision and still keep his sense of direction. After the seventh shot, my left-handed leanings force me around in an angle of ninety degrees without realizing that I have turned at all. Then elated with the wonderful "out" I have finally negotiated, I rise to the surface only to find that I have shot right back through the foursome behind me and lost about sixty yards. I once had a series of these mishaps and spent an hour and a half on one hole continually losing ground. There was an insane asylum across the road from the course and it took my friends quite a while to convince an attendant who happened to see me that I was not an escaped inmate.

There are many other disadvantages that we left-handers must suffer, including the fact that they're building suburban homes closer and closer to the golf courses. The left-hander, when he dubs a shot, always lands in somebody's back yard and this isn't very pleasant when they're cooking codfish.

I think I have made my case clear. What golf really needs is a course where left-handers can be segregated like smallpox patients. It would be simple to lay out one of these courses. A golf architect can take a plan of any well-known course and build it backwards. He may run into a few snags in the locker room. It will be quite a feat of engineering to get the attendant to mix cocktails standing on his head, and the water to run uphill in the shower baths. But trifling difficulties have never stopped the march of progress. Did snags and prejudices stop Lysander J. Lentil when he started to construct the first portable sink, now socially known as the fingerbowl?

# Why There's
# No Crying in Golf

### *by John L. Low*

*Two-time British amateur champion John L. Low (1869-1929) was one of the first to put to paper his thoughts on golf strategy and course design. With the 1903 publication of* Concerning Golf, *he let golfers everywhere in on his thinking.*

Nothing contributes more to the popularity of golf than its almost endless variety. No two courses are the same, even though they be similar in character; no two shots are alike, even though the same distance has to be accomplished.... Every fresh hole we play should teach us some new possibility of using our strokes and suggest to us a further step in the progress of our golfing knowledge.... This variety is a very distinct feature of the game.

Football or cricket grounds, if good, do not vary much from one another. Certain soils, no doubt, lend themselves better to turf-growing than others, and the sticky patches favor the bowlers, but the conformation of the cricket and football field remains the same.

In golf it is quite otherwise; each course has its own features, and each demands a fresh variety of strokes. The play at St. Andrews or Hoylake is quite different from the play at Sandwich — so different that the clubs suitable for the hard turf of the North Country greens would require modification if used on the softer turf of the South Kent course.

The golfer who has grown weary of one set of strokes has only to leave his home green and pay a visit to some other course, and he will find new difficulties to be encountered and have to devise fresh methods of overcoming them. No golfer has ever been forced to say to himself with tears, "There are no more links to conquer."

# A Plea for Indoor Golf

### by P. G. Wodehouse

*Sir Pelham Grenville Wodehouse (1881-1975) was an acknowledged master of modern prose and an admittedly obsessive high-handicapper. "I never win a match," he once admitted. "I spend my life. I never even count my strokes." The creator of Jeeves, Bertie Wooster, and the Oldest Living Member, his many short stories on golf are comic gems — like this trifle, penned just before the '20s began to roar.*

Indoor golf is that which is played in the home. Whether you live in a palace or a hovel, an indoor golf course, be it only of nine holes, is well within your reach. A house offers greater facilities than an apartment, and I have found my game greatly improved since I went to live in the country. I can, perhaps, scarcely do better than give a brief description of the sporting nine-hole course which I have recently laid out in my present residence.

All authorities agree that the first hole on every links should be moderately easy, in order to give the nervous player a temporary and fictitious confidence.

At Wodehouse Manor, therefore, we drive off from the front door — in order to get the benefit of the doormat — down an entry fairway, carpeted with rugs and without traps. The hole — a loving-cup — is just under the stairs; and a good player ought to have no difficulty in doing it in two.

The second hole, a short and simple one, takes you into the telephone booth. Trouble begins with the third, a long dogleg hole through the kitchen into the dining room. This hole is well trapped with table legs, kitchen utensils, and a moving hazard in the person of Clarence the cat, who is generally wandering about the fairway. The hole is under the glass-and-china cupboard, where you are liable to be bunkered if you loft your approach shot excessively.

The fourth and fifth holes call for no comment. They are without traps, the only danger being that you may lose a stroke through hitting the maid if she happens to be coming down the back stairs while you are taking a mashie shot. This is a penalty under the local rule.

The sixth is the indispensable water hole. It is short, but tricky. Teeing off from just outside the bathroom door, you have to loft the ball over the side of the bath, holing out in the little vent pipe at the end where the water runs out.

The seventh is the longest hole on the course. Starting at

the entrance of the best bedroom, a full drive takes you to the head of the stairs, whence you will need at least two more strokes to put you dead on the pin in the drawing room. In the drawing room the fairway is trapped with photograph frames — with glass, complete — these serving as casual water: and anyone who can hole out on the piano in five or under is a player of class. Bogey is six, and I have known even such a capable exponent of the game as my Uncle Reginald, who is plus two on his home links on Park Avenue, to take 27 at the hole. But on that occasion he had the misfortune to be bunkered in a photograph of my Aunt Clara and took no fewer than eleven strokes with his niblick to extricate himself from it.

The eighth and ninth holes are straightforward, and can be done in two and three respectively, provided you swing easily and avoid the canary's cage. Once trapped there, it is better to give up the hole without further effort. It is almost impossible to get out in less than 56, and after you have taken about 30 the bird gets visibly annoyed.

# On the Old Course at St. Andrews

## *by Bernard Darwin*

*You don't need a Charles Darwin to suggest that golfers are a species completely unto their own, but to understand some of the origin of that species, it's worth climbing up another branch of that family tree. Bernard Darwin (1876-1961), Charles's grandson, gave up law to practice golf and became the progenitor of "the golf writer." His prose, as this excerpt from his 1910 classic* The Golf Courses of the British Isles *demonstrates, survives as some of the fittest, and most elegant, in the language. An excellent player, Darwin, on assignment to cover the first Walker Cup matches in 1922, was pressed into service as an emergency replacement for a British team member. He won his match.*

Really to know the links of St. Andrews can never be given to the casual visitor. It is not perhaps necessary to be one of those old gentlemen who tell us at all too frequent intervals that golf was golf in their young days, that we of today are solely occupied in the pur-

> "I AM STILL UNDECIDED AS TO WHICH OF THESE TWO IS THE HARDEST SHOT IN GOLF FOR ME — ANY UNCONCEDED PUTT, OR THE EXPLOSION SHOT OFF THE FIRST TEE. BOTH HAVE CAUSED ME MORE STROKES THAN I CARE TO WRITE ABOUT."
>
> — RING LARDNER

suit of pots and pans, and that Sir Robert Ray, with his tall hat and his graduated series of spoons, would have beaten us, one and all, into the middle of the ensuing week. Such a degree of senile decay is fortunately not essential, but one ought to have known and loved and played over the links for a long while; and I can lay no claims to such knowledge as that. I can speak only as an occasional pilgrim, whose pilgrimages, though always reverent, have been far too few....

There are those who do not like the golf at St. Andrews, and they will no doubt deny any charm to the links themselves, but there must surely be none who will deny a charm to the place as a whole. It may be immoral, but it is delightful to see a whole town given up to golf; to see the butcher and the baker and the candlestick maker shouldering his clubs as soon as his day's work is done and making a dash for the links. There he and his fellows will very possibly get in our way, or we shall get in theirs; we shall often curse the crowd, and wish wholeheartedly that golf was less popular in

St. Andrews. Nevertheless it is that utter self-abandonment to golf that gives the place its attractiveness. What a pleasant spectacle is that home green, fenced in on two sides by a railing, upon which lean various critical observers; and there is the clubhouse on one side, and the clubmaker's shop and the hotels on the other, all full of people who are looking at the putting, and all talking of putts that they themselves holed or missed on that or some other green....

St. Andrews never looks really easy, and never is really easy, for the reason that the bunkers are for the most part so close to the greens. It is possible, of course, to play an approach shot straight on the beeline to the flag, and if we play it to absolute perfection all may go well; but let it only be crooked by so much as a yard, or let the ball, as it often will do, get an unkind kick, and the bunker will infallibly be our portion....

Let not the reader hastily assume that his only difficulty at St. Andrews will be to keep out of the clutches of the bunkers lying close to the greens; he will find plenty more stumbling blocks in his path. There is the matter of length, for instance. The holes, either out or home, do not look very long ... with the wind behind ..., but it is an entirely different matter when we have to play them ... with the wind in our teeth.... There are a great many holes that demand two good shots, as struck by the ordinary mortal; there are three that he cannot reach except with his third, and there are only two that he can reach from the tee, of which one by common consent is the most fiendish short hole in existence. Thus we have two difficulties, that the holes are long, and that there are bunkers close to the greens; now, for a third, those greens are for the most part on beautiful pieces of golfing ground, which by their natural conformation, by their banks and braes and slopes, guard the holes very effectively, even without the aid of the numerous bunkers.... Finally, the turf is very hard, and consequently the greens are apt to take on a keenness that is paralyzing in its intensity.

Having by alarming generalizations induced in the unfortunate stranger a suitably humble frame of mind, the time has now arrived to take him over the course in some detail. The first thing to point out ... is the historic fact that there were once upon a time but nine holes, and that the outgoing and incoming players aimed at the self-same hole upon the self-same green. That state of things has necessarily long passed away, but the result is still to be seen in the fact that most of the greens are actually or in effect double greens, and consequently the two processions of golfers outward- and inward-bound pass close to each other, not without some risk to life and much shouting of "Fore!"

With this preliminary observation, we may tee up our ball in front of the Royal and Ancient Clubhouse for one of the least alarming tee shots in existence. In front of us stretches a vast flat plain, and unless we slice the ball outrageously onto the sea beach, no harm can befall us. At the same time we had much better hit a good shot, because the Swilcan burn guards the green, and we want to carry it and get a four. It is an inglorious little stream enough: we could easily jump over it were we not afraid of looking foolish if we fell in, and yet it catches an amazing number of balls.

The second is a beautiful hole some 400 yards in length, and with the most destructive of pot-bunkers close up against the hole. Here is a case in point, when the attempt to shave narrowly past the bunker involves terrible risks, and it is the part of prudence to play well out to the right...

"AT THE BEGINNING OF A MATCH DO NOT WORRY YOURSELF WITH THE IDEA THAT THE RESULT IS LIKELY TO BE AGAINST YOU. BY REFLECTING THUS UPON THE POSSIBILITIES OF DEFEAT, ONE BECOMES TOO ANXIOUS AND LOSES ONE'S FREEDOM OF STYLE."
— HARRY VARDON

The fifth is the long hole out, when we shall need our three strokes to reach the green, which stands a little above us on a plateau of magnificent dimensions, where we rub shoulders with the incoming couples who are plying the "Hole o' Cross." In ancient days, when the whins were thick and flourishing on the straight road to the hole, the only possible line was away to the left towards the Elysian fields. It was from there, so Mr. James Cunningham has told me, that young Tommy Morris astonished the spectators by taking his niblick, a club that in those days had a face of about the magnitude of a half-crown, wherewith to play a pitch on the green. Till that historic moment no one had ever dreamed of a niblick being used for anything but ordinary spade work....

At the eighth we do at last get a chance of a three, for the hole is a short one — 142 yards long to be precise — and there is a fair measure of room on the green. So far the golf has been very, very good indeed, but with the ninth and tenth come two holes that constitute a small blot on the fair fame of the course. If they were found on some less sacred spot they would be condemned as consisting of a drive and a pitch up and down a flat field. What makes it the sadder is that ready to the architect's hand is a bit of glorious golfing country on the confines of the new course. However, we had better play these two holes in as reverent a spirit as possible and be thankful for two fairly easy fours, because the next is the "short hole in," and we must reserve all our energies for that.

The only consoling thing about the hole is that the green slopes upward, so that it is not quite so easy for the ball to run over it as it otherwise would be. This is really but cold comfort, however, because the danger of going too far is not so imminent as that of not going straight enough. There is one bunker called "Strath," which is to the right, and there is another called the "Shelly Bunker," to the left; there is also another bunker short of Strath to catch the thoroughly short and ineffective ball. The hole is as a rule cut fairly close to Strath, wherefore it behooves the careful man to play well away to the left, and not to take undue risks by going straight for the hole. This may sound pusillanimous, but trouble once begun at this hole may never come to an end till the card is torn into a thousand fragments.... It is a hole to leave behind one with a sigh of satisfaction.

> "YOU GET REWARDED AT THE BOTTOM END OF THE CLUB BY WHAT YOU DO AT THE TOP END."
> — JERRY BARBER

The next hole would in any case fall almost inevitably flat, but the thirteenth, the Hole o' Cross, is a great hole, where having struck two really fine shots and escaped "Walkinshaw's Grave," we may hope to reach the beautiful big plateau green in two and hole out in two more....

Although home is now in sight, there are yet two terribly dangerous holes to be played. First of all we must steer down the perilously narrow space between the "Principal's Nose" and the railway line — the railway line, mark you that is not out-of-bounds, so that there is no limit to the number of strokes that we may spend in hammering vainly at an insensate sleeper. We may, of course, drive safe away to the left, and if our score is a good one we shall be wise to do so, but our approach, as is only fair, will then be the more difficult, and there are bunkers lurking by the greenside.

The seventeenth hole has been more praised and more abused probably than any other hole in the world. It has been called unfair, and by many harder names as well; it has caused champions with a predilection for pitching rather than running

"ALL RIGHT, WHAT WOULD YOUR PAL HOGAN DO IN A SITUATION LIKE THIS?"
— ARNOLD PALMER, FINDING HIS TEE SHOT UNDER A TREE, TO COLUMNIST JIM MURRAY

"HOGAN WOULDN'T BE IN A POSITION LIKE THAT."
— MURRAY BACK TO PALMER

to tear their hair; it has certainly ruined an infinite number of scores. Many like it, most respect it, and all fear it. First there is the tee shot, with the possibility of slicing out-of-bounds into the stationmaster's garden or pulling into various bunkers on the left. Then comes the second, a shot which should not entail immediate disaster, but which is nevertheless of enormous importance as leading up to the third. Finally, there is the approach to that little plateau — in contrast to most of the St. Andrews greens, a horribly small and narrow one that lies between a greedy little bunker on the one side and a brutally hard road on the other. It is so difficult as to make the boldest inclined to approach on the installment system, and yet no amount of caution can do away with the chance of disaster....

After this hole of many disastrous memories, the eighteenth need have no great terrors. We drive over the burn, cross by the picturesque old stone bridge, and avoiding the grosser forms of sin, such as slicing into the windows of Rusack's Hotel, hole out in four, or at most five, under the critical gaze of those that lean on the railings....

# The Golf Holes at Augusta National

*Each of the eighteen holes at Augusta National has a floral or arboreous name that stands in colorful contrast to the stark terror that some holes present to Masters competitors. Picture this:*

*"I was two under par until I got to Camellia. Bogeyed that. Then I was four over par after I played White Dogwood, Golden Bell and Azalea. But it was Red Bud that killed me with my damn triple bogey. Frightening, that Azalea and that damn Red Bud!"*

1. Tea Olive
2. Pink Dogwood
3. Flowering Peach
4. Flowering Crabapple
5. Magnolia
6. Juniper
7. Pampas
8. Yellow Jasmine
9. Carolina Cherry

10. Camellia
11. White Dogwood
12. Golden Bell
13. Azalea
14. Chinese Fir
15. Fire Thorn
16. Red Bud
17. Nandina
18. Holly

# 8

# THE UN–LIE–ABLE PLAY

(ETIQUETTE AND SPORTSMANSHIP)

# What's Good for the Goose...

## *by Art Buchwald*

*A national institution, Buchwald and his satiric visions won the Pulitzer Prize for commentary in 1982, three years after he described this incident which publicly cooked the goose of the duffer who bloodied his scorecard with a birdie. Perhaps only Wodehouse's Oldest Member of the Club could have given this "fowl" episode equal justice.*

A new chapter in the annals of justice — or is it golf — was written last week when a Washington physician was charged with beating a Canada goose to death with his putter on the seventeenth green of the Congressional Country Club.

The charges brought by federal wildlife authorities were originally investigated by the country club's board of directors, but they came to no conclusion as to what really happened. Dr. Sherman A. Thomas, the accused golfer, said that his approach shot to the green hit the goose, one of two hanging around the seventeenth hole. In his medical opinion, the goose was in such agony from the blow of the ball that the doctor decided to put it out of its misery. Instead of pulling the plug on the goose, he struck it several times with his putting iron, thus performing the first mercy killing of a feathered bird on any golf course since the game was invented.

But there is another version, and this is the reason the wildlife people have preferred charges. Dr. Thomas, according to an eyewitness, was about to putt when the goose honked. This, the witness maintains, so enraged the physician that he attacked the goose with his putter and killed the bird.

The doctor is charged with "knowingly killing a goose out of season" and also with being "illegally in possession of a dead Canada goose." Even had Dr. Thomas killed the goose when the hunting season was on, he would still have been in violation of the law, as the Bird Act specifies you can only go after geese with shotguns, bows and arrows, falcons and goshawks.

Putters are out of the question.

If the doctor is found guilty he could receive a maximum sentence of six months in jail and a fine of $500.

So much for killing one's goose.

The main question is how does this affect the game of golf?

> "I AM STUMPED WHEN IT COMES TO SAYING WHICH IS THE HARDEST SHOT IN GOLF FOR ME, BUT I KNOW THE EASIEST ONE — THE FIRST SHOT AT THE NINETEENTH HOLE."
> — W. C. FIELDS

Every golfer I heard out gave me a different interpretation of the rules.

One said, "I believe that Dr. Thomas should have been penalized one stroke for each time he hit the goose."

But someone else in the locker room disagreed. "No, you cannot be penalized no matter how many times you strike at the bird, providing you don't move your ball. From what I understand, Thomas approached the ball; the goose honked; he left the ball on the green, and started to swing his putter at the Canada's head. It might be considered illegal bird killing, but it certainly is not illegal golf."

"Wait a minute," another duffer said. "Thomas's story was that his ball accidentally hit the goose on his approach shot to the green. Therefore, although he had to play his ball from the spot where it fell after it struck the bird, he was still under par when he attacked the goose with his putter."

"But why the putter?" someone asked. "Wouldn't it have been more merciful if he had done it with a five-iron?"

"It's all right for us to sit here in the locker room and Monday-morning quarterback Thomas's choice of irons, but I believe you have to be in his golf shoes before you can say which club he should have used. I might have killed the goose with a driver. You might have killed him with a niblick, but Thomas was right there and decided a putter was all that was needed."

"I believe we need a club ruling on this. Today it's Thomas, tomorrow it could be one of us. I want to know exactly how many shots I am permitted before I get a birdie."

"As long as we're at it," another chap said, "I would like to ask the grounds committee what a Canada goose was doing there in the first place. Correct me if I'm wrong, but aren't Canadians forbidden from using the course during the hours when members are playing?"

"I believe there is a bylaw on it," someone replied. "But let's find out the exact wording as to when you stuff a goose and when you putt it."

# The Inequity of Golf

### by Charles Blair Macdonald

*The first United States national amateur champion, Chicago's Macdonald (1855-1939) went off to study at St. Andrews University in 1872 and returned two years later with a pretty good game, taught by Old Tom Morris himself. Considered the father of American golf course design, Macdonald's imprint stamps the Greenbriar, the loop at Yale University, and his masterpiece, the National Golf Links on Long Island. He concluded his lovely 1928 volume* Scotland's Gift — Golf *with a series of* Rambling Thoughts, *one of which rambles gracefully here.*

So many people preach equity in golf. Nothing is so foreign to the truth. Does any human being receive what he conceives as equity in his life? He has got to take the bitter with the sweet, and as he forges through all the intricacies and inequalities which life presents, he proves his mettle. In golf the cardinal rules are arbitrary and not founded on eternal justice. Equity has nothing to do with the game itself. If founded on eternal justice the game would be deadly dull to watch or play.

The essence of the game is inequality, as it is in humanity. The conditions which are meted out to the players, such as inequality of the ground, cannot be governed by a green committee with the flying divots of the players or their footprints in the bunkers. Take your medicine where you find it and don't cry. Remember that the other fellow has got to meet exactly the same inequalities....

I do not like to refer to people who are always trying to tinker with the rules of the game. They are to me heretics. One group of men makes an effort to increase the size of the hole; another group thinks putting too important, and desire to call a stroke on the putting green one-half stroke. God forbid!

If you have a good sporting time, for heaven's sake don't try too much to improve it. Your business is not to improve the game but to *improve your play.*

> "ALWAYS USE THE CLUB THAT TAKES THE LEAST OUT OF YOU. PLAY WITH A LONG IRON INSTEAD OF FORCING YOUR SHOT WITH A SHORT IRON. NEVER SAY, 'OH, I THINK I CAN REACH IT WITH SUCH AND SUCH A CLUB.' THERE OUGHT NEVER TO BE ANY QUESTION OF YOUR REACHING IT, SO USE THE NEXT MORE POWERFUL CLUB IN ORDER THAT YOU WILL HAVE A LITTLE IN HAND."
>
> — HARRY VARDON

# Disease, Diagnosis and Cure

### by Timothy Ward

*Call it human nature, or just call it golf, but for as long as we've been whacking away at small balls with sticks and tallying up our totals, we've been prey to various afflictions and disorders that gnaw into our scorecards like hungry, flesh-eating bacteria. In 1899, writing in* Golfing Magazine, *Ward identified and examined in some detail an epidemic malady that he dubbed "Mendacitis Anarithmetica."*

This is a very strange complaint and is by no means confined to either sex.... The chief observable symptom is a total suppression of the sense of strict accuracy, coupled with an absolute inability to make two and two anything more than three. Some wonderful scores have thus been achieved, not of malice prepense, but of sheer want of memory. It is also a peculiarity of such patients that though in reality perfectly conversant with the rules, they are ready to forget them whenever it may be conducive to the making of a good score for them to do so. They will even, in playing through the green, not be too particular as to remove twigs, etc., upon which their ball may be actually lying, and if such removal cause the ball to roll out of its position, even say for six or eight inches, they will not be concerned or even disposed to incur the penalty provided for such illegal performances. If you do not catch them in flagrante delicto, nothing is said; if you do, they invariably plead ignorance of the rule, even though you may have on many previous occasions called their attention to and explained it.

In bunkers, as a matter of habit and precaution, they invariably leave the truth outside — indeed, I have seen them after having landed their tee shot in the bunker specially provided for such players, emerge, almost triumphantly therefrom, after about five or six minutes solid hard work, and heard them say, with a beaming countenance, as if flushed with triumph, "Two!" or if in a very gracious mood, "Three!" when you know really that these figures represent dozens and not units as they would have you believe.

Finally, according to their reckoning they may do the hole — a bogey six — in five, and win it, as they think, from you; and when, as if by accident, you examine their ball, point out at least ten or twelve separate and distinct mementoes of the niblick, and remind them that the ball was a new one at that tee, they frankly avow that they "cannot make that out, but

"EVERY GAME OF GOLF THAT HAS EVER BEEN PLAYED — WHETHER THE MEDAL WAS 68 OR 168 — HAS TAKEN PLACE ON A GOLF COURSE THAT MEASURED EIGHT INCHES MORE OR LESS. I ARRIVED AT THE DIMENSIONS OF THIS GOLF COURSE BY TAKING A RULER AND MEASURING MY OWN HEAD FROM BACK TO FRONT. OF COURSE, EVERY GAME OF GOLF IS PLAYED — EVERY SHOT IS PLAYED — IN YOUR MIND BEFORE THE BALL ACTUALLY STARTS ON ITS WAY."

— EDDIE LOOS

perhaps it was six and not five after all."

In competitions they are rather dangerous. They think all the time that you are trying to cheat them, so that you may win yourself, quite regardless of the fact that in order to play a good game, all your energies should be devoted to that end, instead of being constantly required in the well-nigh hopeless task of rectifying their imperfect memory. Sometimes on putting greens, a player of this type has been known quite accidentally to move the ball an inch or more, whereupon without your having said a word, he will turn round and say to you, almost angrily, "That wasn't a stroke, the ball never moved." Should you show him how far it moved from its original position, he will probably say, "Oh! That doesn't count."

There is only one way to deal with players of this class.

Firmly implant on your memory, and on your caddie's, the resting place of the ball after each stroke, and as firmly but courteously, insist on the total number being placed on the card, without allowing any discussion after, say, the first three holes or so. You can generally convince the patient about these, and when he sees that you are watching and counting, and that the caddies are doing so as well, he will probably begin to count accurately himself, which greatly simplifies matters.

# The Original Thirteen

*The original* Articles & Laws in Playing at Golf *were established by the Honorable Company of Edinburgh Golfers in 1744 to govern an impending tournament on the Links at Leith. Adopted a decade later by the Society of St. Andrews Golfers, they have, of course, mushroomed over time. Still, what remains most compelling about these foundation rules is just how much the game played today can be found within the first twelve; consider No. 13 something more on the order of a local adjustment.*

1. You must tee your ball within one club's length of hole.
2. Your tee must be on the ground.
3. You are not to change the ball you strike off the tee.
4. You are not to remove Stones, Bones or any Break Club, for sake of playing your ball, except upon the Fair Green and that only within a club's length of your ball.
5. If your Ball come among watter or any wattery filth, you are at liberty to take out your Ball and, bringing it behind the hazard and teeing it, you may play it with any club and allow your Adversary a Stroke, for so getting out your ball.

6. If your balls be found anywhere touching one another you are to lift the first ball, till you play the last.

7. At Holing, you are to play your Ball honestly for the Hole, and not play upon your Adversary's Ball, not lying in your way to the Hole.

8. If you should lose your Ball, by its being taken up, or any other way you are to go back to the Spot, where you struck last, and drop another Ball, and allow your adversary a stroke for the misfortune.

9. No man at Holing his Ball is to be allowed, to mark his way to the Hole with his club or anything else.

10. If a Ball be stopp'd by any person, Horse, Dog or anything else, the Ball so stopp'd must be played where it lyes.

11. If you draw your Club, in order to Strike and proceed so far in the Stroke, as to be bringing down your Club: If then your Club shall break, in any way, it is to be Accounted a Stroke.

12. He whose Ball lyes farthest from the Hole is obliged to play first.

13. Neither Trench, Ditch or Dyke, made for the presentation of the Links, nor the Scholar's Holes or the Soldier's Lines, Shall be accounted a Hazard. But the ball is to be taken out and tee'd and play'd with any iron club.

# Keep the Rules and They Keep You

## *by Colman McCarthy*

*Over the course of a distinguished career, longtime* Washington Post *columnist Colman McCarthy has written much on questions of ethics, religion and golf, all of which he managed to combine in this marvelous essay from the '70s. He now directs the Center for Teaching Peace in Washington, D.C.*

Forty-one rules aren't so many — St. Benedict had seventy-three to keep the brethren on the straight and narrow. Yet, many golfers who have mastered the runics of the swing have not bothered much to master the simplicities of the rules, kept current by the vigilant fathers of the United States Golf Association and the Royal and Ancient Golf Club of St. Andrews, Scotland.

Most golfers are quite content with a mere acquaintance

of the few basics that keep the game civilized — no kicking your opponent's ball into the rough when he's not looking, no stealing the honor on the tee — but after that, it often seems that anything goes. This attitude of abandon is more fitting for sports in which blood lust is an asset — like sparring with broken pool cues. Golf courses are havens for the nonhostile, where umpires and referees are not needed because the players themselves know the rules and obey them.

Is there a finer joy, short of clearing a pond by inches, than assessing an opponent two strokes who (as though playing croquet) strikes your ball on the putting green (breaching rule 35), cleans a muddy ball on the fairway (violating rule 23) or marks a line of flight on a blind shot over a hill (breaking rule 9)?

When calling attention to these rules and their unpleasant penalties, be prepared for pouting or fuming. You will be accused of unmentionable practices. But think of yourself, at such times, as Abraham Lincoln walking back those ten miles (a distance somewhat exceeding twenty-seven holes of golf) to return the penny. Your mission is honesty.

When someone tells you that you lead a dull life, deep in the sopor of rules and laws, tell them Arnold Palmer probably won the 1958 Masters because he knew the rules. On the par-three twelfth hole of the final round, on a soggy day in Augusta, Palmer flew the green and the ball imbedded in the back apron. A dispute arose when Palmer claimed he was

> "THE BALL DOESN'T CARE HOW POSITIVE YOU ARE THINKING WHEN YOU HIT IT WITH A PUTTER MOVING AND AIMED IN THE WRONG DIRECTION."
> — DAVE PELZ

entitled to a free drop; the official in the green jacket said no. Each was satisfied when Palmer played both a provisional ball, on which he scored three and his first ball, on which he took a five. The tournament rules men then huddled and determined that Palmer was entitled to a free drop and the three stood....

The St. Andrews Scots who wrote the early rules were Calvinists who believed that although a golf course may look like paradise, its users are potential wrongdoers. Shadows of sneakiness loom in us all, however sunny an aspect we present on the first tee. What is to prevent, say, a threesome of professionals from rigging their scores by signing cards two or three strokes lower than their actual tallies? Strikingly, it has always been one of the game's distinctions that the golf tour has never had a major cheating scandal. In 1972 Jane Blalock was accused of moving her ball in the rough by some other women on the tour, but the charges were never proven. In fact, she sued, in turn, the Ladies Professional Golfers Association and won a judgment that the LPGA was in violation of the Sherman Antitrust Act for not allowing her to compete in tournaments while her case was pending. In amateur golf, only the Deepdale scandal of the mid-1950s (in which phony handicaps were used by some of the contestants) is a splotch on the sport's purity. I have played with board members of corporations who lied, stole and cheated their way to the top, but who on the fairways were watchful of golf's rules and its etiquette. .

Watchfulness goes to the heart of the matter, or at least to the aorta. It is not a great strain, for example, to avoid walking in the line of another's putt. Small effort is needed to keep from moving behind a player as he addresses the ball. And only moderate self-control is required to refrain from hitting into the foursome ahead. All that these standards of basic etiquette ask is that we simply be watchful of the other player, so that what we do on the golf course doesn't make it harder for our partners.

As a boy, I made a point of learning the rules. I would study them in the caddie yard while waiting to be assigned a loop. And, indeed, how often I came to use them. During the course of a round, I would watch closely whoever had matches against those I was caddieing for. When I saw a violation, I would call aside my employer and tell him what his opponent had just done. Usually, my man would be glad to get the facts and take action. Occasionally, though, my information was rejected. It would be too embarrassing, some thought. Others feared a stink. Some doubted that the rules made sense. But these were the exceptions. In time, I came to be sought out as a caddie, because my services went beyond merely carrying the clubs and attending the pin....

The point at which many golfers walk away from the rules is when they opt for preferred lies. The advantages of winter rules were intended to apply only when the earth is craggy, pocked by the harshness of the cold and other rudenesses of the winter weather. Such conditions rarely prevail midsummer. Yet, the winter rules player counters that golf is hard enough without enduring the torment of uncivil real estate; if your Titleist lands in a vulgar piece of turf, move it to a more chaste spot. But rule 16 applies in all seasons: "The ball shall be played as it lies and shall not be purposely touched except that the player may, without penalty, touch his ball with his club in the act of addressing it and except as otherwise provided in the rules of local rules."

The challenge of accepting whatever lie we get is fundamental to the pleasures of golf. To accept the rub of the green, even when we must cross it against the grain, is to bring an objectivity to our play that refreshes the spirit. Once when I had the miffy luck of landing a tee shot in a divot hole, my companion called out, "Move the ball, it's OK. When I land in a divot I'll move mine." How tempting it was — to nudge the ball an inch or two to a tuft of grass waiting since the fourth day of creation for a golf ball to land. But who needs to go easy on themselves while at play? By accepting the conditions of turf on the fairways, you gather respect for yourself. When someone tells you, "Move the ball, it's only a game," answer, "No thanks." It's because golf is a game that we can accept its full reality.

In the end, some will always take the preferred lie, as others will ignore the sanctions of other rules. Fidelity to the rules is an acquired skill, and only the few who work at it experience its pleasures. For those who wish to bend the rules, there are always those putt-putt courses next to the truck stops. There, they can shout and stomp until their larynxes loosen when they miss that ten-footer off the sideboard. Amid the traffic and fumes, what could be more appropriate?

# Golf in Times of War

*As a game, golf is perfectly willing to acknowledge war, but still insists on its right to play through. While England was being bombed in World War II, Major G. L. Edsell, secretary of St. Mellons Golf and Country Club, set up these rules designed to accommodate play during the conflagration, which were then adopted throughout the nation.*

1. Players are asked to collect the bomb and shell splinters to save these causing damage to the mowers.

2. In competitions, during gunfire or while bombs are falling, players may take shelter without penalty for ceasing play.

3. The positions of known delayed-action bombs are marked by red and white flags placed at reasonably, but not guaranteed, safe distance from the bombs.

4. Shell and/or bomb splinters on the greens may be moved without penalty. On fairways or in bunkers within a club's

length of a ball they may be moved without penalty and no penalty shall be incurred if a ball is thereby caused to move accidentally.

5. A ball moved by enemy action may be replaced as near as possible to where it lay, or if lost or destroyed, a ball may be dropped no nearer the hole without penalty.

6. A ball lying in any crater may be lifted and dropped not nearer the hole, preserving the line to the hole, without penalty.

7. A player whose stroke is affected by the simultaneous explosion of a bomb or shell, or by machine-gun fire, may play another ball from the same place. Penalty one stroke.

# Is Mulligan the Metaphor for the Clinton Presidency?

*By Don Van Natta Jr.*

*It is one of life's accepted axioms that beacons of morality off the golf course sometimes act like virtual felons on it, but the corollary is even harsher: those who improve their lie on the course most assuredly resort to the lie — and the cheat and steal — off of it.* The New York Times's *Don Van Natta Jr. filed this addendum to the scorecard following a presidential round on Martha's Vineyard in August of 1999. In fairness, it should be pointed out that the Secret Service traditionally frowns on the Commander-in-Chief playing out of the trees because assassins may be lurking. Worse, the real killers O. J. constantly searches for on golf courses just might be hiding in the woods.*

President Clinton stepped up to the first tee at Farm Neck Golf Club the other day and shanked the ball into the wrong fairway. "Aw, I killed it," the president blurted to himself. "I need help."

Without hesitation, Clinton fished for another ball out of his pocket, placed it on the tee and lined up a second shot. In golf parlance, the do-over is known as a mulligan, a benign term for a shot not endorsed by the U.S. Golf Association. It is common among weekend duffers, who will gladly take one or even a handful of do-overs if their fellow players assent.

But Clinton never asked the permission of anyone in his foursome, which included Senator Frank Lautenberg, Democrat-New Jersey. Apparently being president means never having to say double bogey. His second shot mimicked the crooked path of the first, veering onto an adjacent fairway. "Aw, I did it again," Clinton said, stomping toward his golf cart.

Indeed, the president does it again and again and again. He grants himself bushels of mulligans — off the tee, usually, but presidential mulligans have also been witnessed while Clinton was ankle-deep in sand or lost in a thicket of evergreen trees. Clinton jokes that he gives "presidential pardons" to his errant golf balls....

The mulligan presents itself as the perfect metaphor for the Clinton presidency. The voters have given the Comeback Kid more than one mulligan. Clinton was granted a second chance by the Senate in February after the House impeached him for his behavior in the Monica Lewinsky matter. And it can be assumed that Hillary Rodham Clinton has given Clinton a few mulligans too.

> "IN GOLF, AS IN LIFE, THE ATTEMPT TO DO SOMETHING IN ONE STROKE THAT NEEDS TWO IS APT TO RESULT IN TAKING THREE."
> — WALTER CAMP

Most past presidents were golf purists who wouldn't contemplate even asking for a mulligan (the term's derivation is obscure), let alone taking one. President George Bush apparently never took a do-over. For him, it was more important to put the game out of its misery; he once bragged that he raced through eighteen holes in one hour, forty-two minutes.

John F. Kennedy, probably the best golfer to occupy the White House this century, did not need to take mulligans. Richard M. Nixon, on the other hand, was known to kick the ball out of the rough to give himself a better lie.

Golf was also a defining metaphor of Dwight D. Eisenhower's presidency. Ike spent so much time puttering around the links that his diversion symbolized his entire era of placid postwar prosperity and conservatism.

Clinton's game symbolizes something else. In his book *Shadow: Five Presidents and the Legacy of Watergate*, Bob Woodward states that former President Gerald R. Ford, an avid golfer, was disgusted after watching Clinton repeatedly take mulligans during a round in Colorado in 1993.

After playing eighteen holes with Ford and pro golf great Jack Nicklaus, Clinton told reporters he had shot an 80.

This claim apparently infuriated Ford and Nicklaus.

Woodward writes: "Nicklaus leaned over to Ford and whispered in disgust, 'Eighty with fifty floating mulligans.'"

A golfer who routinely takes mulligans is rarely taxed by the game's cruelties. A handicap aided by second chances allows the golfer to maintain an optimistic outlook on life. On the other hand, one who never takes mulligans cannot help brooding about the game's harshness and unfairness.

Former Senator Bob Dole, who does not play golf, attempted to transform the mulligan into an issue during the waning days of his losing presidential campaign in 1996. "I don't know whether he shot an 83 or a 283 or a 483," Dole growled in response to the president's claim that he shot an 83 in Albuquerque, New Mexico. "You'll never really know."

On a glorious spring day in May, Clinton appeared incapable of getting the kinks out of his swing on the first tee at the Andrews Air Force Base course. He took one mulligan. Then another. And then another. Each shot was spectacularly ugly, zigzagging this way and that. Finally, the president was satisfied with his fourth shot, which managed to land in the fairway.

Paul Bedard, a writer with *U.S. News & World Report* who witnessed the flurry of mulligans, called it "the highest-ever number of cheater's shots the First Duffer has taken before witnesses."

But beyond the first tee there are few witnesses. Reporters, armed with scorecards and little pencils, are forbidden from following the presidential foursome around the course. Thus, even though Clinton is far along the back nine of his presidency, it has been almost impossible to document how many mulligans he takes during any single round.

Terence McAuliffe, a friend and frequent golfing partner of Clinton's, vouched for the president's claim that he grants presidential pardons only to balls hit from the first tee. "And only rarely," he added. McAuliffe said his matches with the president are far too competitive for either one of them to indulge in a multitude of mulligans.

"It's a dogfight out there," he said. "He is as competitive about golf as he is about life. He doesn't like to lose, and neither do I. Neither one of us will give the other guy a break."

Despite such assurances, cynics in the gallery continue to believe that the president's scores — he claims to shoot around 80 and as low as 75 — are enhanced by at least a half-dozen mulligans. Sure, the president is a pretty good golfer, the cynics say. He's just not that good.

Skepticism is, of course, understandable. Clinton, after all, claimed that he did not inhale, and that he did not have sexual relations with that woman. Why wouldn't the president also put the spin on his golf score?

Rick Reilly, a senior writer for *Sports Illustrated* who played with the president in 1996, recalled that Clinton took just one mulligan at the Congressional Country Club in Bethesda, Maryland, before carding an impressive 82. "He hit a lot of mad balls — he'd chunk one, or skull one, and he'd get mad and hit another shot, but then he'd always play the first bad shot," said Reilly. "He had a reporter and a photographer with him, so he was really on his best behavior."

During his Martha's Vineyard vacation in August 1997, Clinton hammered three straight tee shots into the woods near the first fairway. Afterward, White House press secretary Mike McCurry dutifully reported that the president had carded a seven-over-par 79. Journalists were aghast. They immediately demanded to know how many mulligans the president had taken.

> "GOLF HAS MADE MORE LIARS OUT OF PEOPLE THAN INCOME TAX."
> — WILL ROGERS

McCurry, as they say, "declined to comment."

At the time, John Omicinski, a commentator for the Gannett News Service, admonished, "In golf, as in life, he's got to learn to take his punishment and learn from his mistakes, rather than covering them up." That was five months before the world was introduced to Monica Lewinsky.

This month, Clinton presented the Medal of Freedom to Jimmy Carter and his wife, Rosalynn. Carter seized the opportunity to inform Clinton about what to expect after he leaves the White House in January 2001.

"You'll be able to play golf without any telephoto lens focusing on your stroke," Carter, a nongolfer, told the president. "But there is a downside: I understand golfing partners don't give as many mulligans" to ex-presidents.

Clinton smiled, but it was a slightly pained smile. Before long, he will have to relinquish his job and all its privileges.

# Shush!!!
# An Authority on Athaletics
# Makes a Suggestion

### *by Ring Lardner*

*One of the first of the great American sports writers, Ringgold Wilmer Lardner (1885-1933) was funny and cynical. His most celebrated work,* You Know Me, Al, *a 1916 collection of short stories that essentially combine to form an epistolary novel, broke stylistic ground in its masterly use of the vernacular. He applied the same techniques — bad grammar, misspellings, and all — to golf in this 1921 contribution to* The American Golfer.

To the Editor:

I want to call your tension to something about golf that has been ranking in my bosom for a long wile and I would have said something about it yrs. ago only I thought a man of your brains and intelligents would take steps, but I suppose you are afraid of the Old Guard amist your readers and scared of offending them, but where they's a principal involved I never fail to speak out my mind and my friends say I have done it so often that it is what you might call spoken out.

Well, it looks to me like they was room for improvement in the game and when I say the game I don't mean my game but the game itself as gotten up by St. Andrew and Simon Peter his brother and the next time the rules committee gets together I wished they would make a change in the code witch looks to me to be a whole lot more important than takeing the endearing terms out of tennis or makeing a pitcher keep his finger nails pared so as he can't scratch baseball or self.

According to what I have read golf is suppose to be the most sociable game in the world and in my $1.50 dictionary one of the definitions of sociable is "suited for, or characterized by, much conversation." Well, then, why and the he-ll don't they mend the golf rules so as a man can talk wile they're playing? Instead of witch, if you say a word to a regular golfer wile he is makeing a shot, why the first thing he will do is suffer a nervous break down and then he will give you a dirty look and likely as not he will pick up his toys and walk off the links, as I have nicknamed them. And when you ask somebody what was the idear they will tell you that your ethics is rancid and you must be scum, because how can a man concentrate on their shot when somebody is makeing remarks at them. And if you was in the gallery at the national amateur and even wispered wile Bobby Ouimet was trying to run down a millimeter putt, why the head linesman would reach in his hip pocket for a sawed off niblick and knock you for a safety.

Well, gents, I have seen a good many different kinds of athaletics and took a small part in a few of them and I ask you as man to man what other event is they where comments is barred?

"Yes," you will say, "but they's no other sport where a man has got to concentrate on what they are doing. If your mind is distracted wile you are playing golf you're gone."

How true.

And now leave us suppose that Ty Cobb is up in the ninth inning of a ball game with two out and the score 7 to 4 vs. Detroit like it usually is and Young and Bush on base. Well, the bench warmers on the other club is yelling "Pop up, Ty! You been a good old wagon but you done broke down." And the catcher is wispering "What shall I have him throw up here, Ty? Do you want a slow ball?" And the boys in the stands is hollering "Strike the big cheese out, Lefty. He's through."

But all this don't worry Ty because he is thinking to himself "I mustn't forget to send my laundry out when I get back to the hotel." His mind ain't on the game at all and when Lefty throws one up there, why it's just from force of habit that he swings and next thing you know Felsch is beating it back to the left center field fence and Jackson is getting set to make the relay. But suppose Ty had been thinking about that next pitch instead of his shirts, why the uproar would of give him neurasthenia and they'd of had to send the trainer up to hit for him.

Or suppose for inst. they's a horse race and they are comeing down the strech and Vagabond the favorite is out in front and the second horse is Willie the Wisp that's 20 to 1 and a lot of waiters has a bet down on him and they all begin screaming "Come on Willie" so loud that Vagabond can't help from hearing them, but he don't even look up as he is thinking about a couple of library books that he promised to bring home to his mare.

Or you take what happened down to Toledo last 4 of July. Dempsey lept up and crowned Jessica in the left eye and Jessica suddenly set down but he got up again and sixty thousand and no hundreds larnyxs was shreeking "Kill the big dog, Jack!" and as I recall it, instead of the remarks bothering Dempsey, why he hit Jessica again with the same Gen. results and I would of swore he was concentrateing, but I found out afterwards that he was trying to figure out weather he would have veal chops or a steak for supper. Otherwise he would of raised his hand unlocked and told the referee that he wouldn't go on unlest the fans shut up their d-m noise.

Or leave us consider that extra inning game that wound up in Europe a couple yrs. ago and they was a guy name Frank Foch or something that was suppose to be figureing out how to put on the finishing touchs to it and he was setting down with a map in front of him, but the Germans kept on shooting Big Bertha and Little Eva with the loud pedal on, so finely a orderly come in and asked Mr. Foch if the noise bothered him. And Mr. Foch says "Oh no. It might if I was rapped up in what I am doing. But I was just wondering if I would look better with my mustache off or on, so let them keep on shooting." So it looks like if Mr. Foch had of been really forced to think about the job they had wished on him the Germans would probably be in Harrisburg by this time, changeing engines....

Now in regards to golf itself leave me give you a couple of incidence that happened to me personly witch will show that the boys who crabs against a little sociability is making a mountain climber out of a mole trap. Well, once I was playing out to Riverside near Chi with Albert Seckel and he was giveing me seven and no hundreds strokes per hole and when we came to the last tee we was even up. Well, the last hole was about 260 yds. but you had to drive over the Blue Ridge Mts. of Virginia and you couldn't see the green from the tee and if you didn't get your drive over the Mts. you was utterly lost. Well, for some reason another Seck had the honor and just as he was going to drive, I says "I hope you don't miss the ball entirely" so he drove onto the green and went down in two.

And down to Toledo last July, a few days before Willard became an acrobat, I and Rube Goldberg met in a match game out to Inverness and we was playing for a buck a hole and my caddy was Harry Witwer and he had broughten along a alarm clock and when we would get on the green, witch was seldom, why just as Rube was going to putt, Harry would set off the alarm, and Rube got so nervous that on the 15th. hole Harry throwed my towel into the ring and I was seven down.

> "THE GOOD PLAYER SWINGS THROUGH THE BALL WHILE THE AWKWARD PLAYER HITS AT IT."
> — KEN VENTURI

So all and all, Mr. Editor, I say pass a rule makeing it legal to open your clam when you feel like it and leave us forget this old obsleet law of silent golf witch was gotten up in Scotland where they wouldn't no more talk for nothing than Harry Lauder would sing for the same price. But weather the rule is past or no, when I am playing at golf I am going to say what I want to when I want to and if my oppts. don't like my ethics, why they's showers in the locker room.

Yours Truely,

# Of Nerve and Cordiality

## by Horace G. Hutchinson

*The very definition of the 19th-century sporting gentleman, Hutchinson (1859-1932) was a prolific essayist and one helluva golfer. On the links, he won back-to-back British Amateur titles in 1886 and 1887, and once placed as high as sixth in the Open. He regularly published his thoughts on golf, cricket, shooting, and angling — even on dreams and Sir Walter Scott — and, most enduringly, edited several volumes of the prestigious* Badminton Library of Sports and Pastimes. *He naturally included several of his own efforts in Badminton's* Golf, *published in 1890.*

O f all the games in which the soul of the Anglo-Saxon delights, there is perhaps none which is a severer test of that mysterious quality called "nerve" than the game of golf. It is a game in which a very great deal is apt to depend upon a single stroke — indeed, upon each single stroke throughout the round — and it is at the same time a game which calls for delicately measured strokes, and consequently, for steadiness and control of hand.

"I cannot understand it at all," a famous tiger-slayer was once heard to exclaim, in desperation. "I have shot tigers in India, knowing that my life depended upon the steadiness of my aim, and could swear

> "NINETY PERCENT OF SHORT PUTTS DON'T GO IN."
> — YOGI BERRA

that the ball would go true through the heart; but here is a wretched little putt, a foot and a half long, and I miss it out of very nervousness!"

Singularly enough, it is just those short little putts — those which there is no excuse for missing, and which, in practice, we should infallibly hole, almost without taking aim — that are the great trials of nerve in the big match. The somewhat longer putts are far less trying, and it is just because there is no excuse for missing that our too-active imaginations picture to us how foolish we shall look if we fail, and thus suggest to us a sufficient cause for failure. It is very silly, but it is very human.

Is there any means, then, to be found by which we may cultivate confidence, and silence our morbid imaginings? In a great degree, confidence depends upon health, and upon the spontaneous, harmonious action of eye and hand. We all know how, on those black days when eye and hand are not working well together, purely imaginary difficulties are apt to present themselves upon the smoothest surface of the simplest putt. How rubs and depressions, which are invisible to every eye except our own, appear as insurmountable obstacles, though they have no existence outside of our fancy. Nevertheless, if we fancy our molehill a mountain, we shall need all sorts of scaling ladders and alpenstocks....

\* \* \*

In connection with the game of golf there are certain points of etiquette which, though not of such a nature as to fall within the jurisdiction of written law, are pretty accurately defined by the sanction of custom. Breach of these observances is not punished by the loss of the hole or of a stroke, but rather by the loss of social status in the golfing world. You do not exact an immediate penalty from him who thus outrages *les convenances;* but in your heart of hearts you propose to yourself the severest of all forms of punishment, viz. never to play with him again.

Of all delinquents against the unwritten code, the grossest offender is perhaps he who stands over you, with triumph spiced with derision as you labor in a bunker, and aggressively counts your score aloud. The act of ostentatiously coming out of his own path to look at you is, of itself, almost on the boundary line between good and bad form. Apart from the indecent gloating over your misfortunes which such conduct on his part would seem to imply, it also contains the infinitely more offensive suggestion of a suspicion of your possible unfair dealing when shielded by the bunker's cliff from his espionage. But when he goes the length of audibly counting up your unhappy efforts, with undisguised satisfaction as the sum increases, you can scarcely look upon it otherwise than as an impugnment either of your arithmetic or of your honesty....

> "BASEBALL REVEALS CHARACTER. GOLF EXPOSES IT."
>
> — ERNIE BANKS

Possibly next upon the little list of ... delinquents against the unwritten code of golf etiquette comes he who complains outrageously of the good luck which falls to his opponent's share. We all know that there is a great deal of luck in the game; but we also know, in moments of sober reflection, that on the whole the balance of luck, good or bad, for us or against us, hangs very nearly even. Complaints of one's own bad luck are in infinitely bad taste. But this class of offense is nothing compared with aggressive outcries against the good fortune of an opponent. If circumstances can aggravate a sin so intrinsically evil, it is even more criminal to complain of the good luck that befalls him with whom you are partnered in a scoring competition than your antagonist in a hand-to-hand match. Generally recognized etiquette goes so far as a kind sympathy and interest in the efforts of your partner for the medal round. A community of trials make you feel in a measure dependent upon each other like fellow knights errant in a world peopled with monsters in the shape of all the other competitors. Usually a man is generous enough to feel that if he does not himself win, he would prefer the victory of his partner to that of any other; and when his own fortunes have become desperate, he will lend that partner all the comfort of his sympathy and moral support. This is less the result of the prospect of any little reflected glory than of a genuine fellow-feeling for one passing through the same vale of bunkers as oneself.

Nevertheless you cannot expect your partner's grief for your unmerited misfortunes to be as poignant as your own. This would be pushing altruism to an excess incompatible with that degree of egoism which Mr. Herbert Spencer assures us to be indispensable in this world in its present state of imperfection....

# 9

# CLUBS, COURSES, AND CLUBS

(THE INFRASTRUCTURE)

# Why Your New Driver Cost So Much ...

All right, you've finally broken down and purchased that big, beautiful, heavily endorsed, brand-name atomic driver with the next-generation flexible shaft you've been salivating over ever since you saw a couple of tour pros, emblazoned with the manufacturer's logo, use it to rocket their drives a good 320 yards down the middle of the fairway. Since you couldn't wait for it to go on sale— who would willingly postpone some extra oomph off the tee? — you thrillingly paid the retail freight: $400.

What exactly did you pay for?

According to established industry percentages, this is what it cost the manufacturer to put that piece of heavy artillery in your hands:

BUILDING THE CLUB

Club head material (raw metal) . . . . . . . . . . . $30.00

Club head labor (overhead included) ......... 78.40
Shaft raw materials ..................... 14.00
Shaft assembly labor (overhead included) ..... 33.20
Club assembly labor (overhead included) ..... 25.20

Total cost to build the club ........... $180.80


SELLING THE CLUB

Sales representatives .................... $20.00
Marketing and advertising ................ 48.00
Player contracts ........................ 32.00
Facilities costs ......................... 19.20
Warranty and demo expenses .............. 8.00
Retail margins .......................... 92.00

Total cost to sell the club ............ $219.20

The bottom line is that 45 percent of the club cost goes into the club's manufacture, and 55 percent into its sale, but not a single persimmon was sacrificed in the process.

—J. S.

# ... And Where To Make the Most of It

Now that you've got that state-of-the-art, nuclear-powered driver, the 250 yards you're rocketing it just doesn't seem good enough. You want more. When distance is an issue, is there a golfer breathing who isn't just a little greedy? You want to milk out every precious inch you can. But you've tried everything — different balls, longer takeaway, adjustments in tempo — and you still can't bust through the 250-yard marker.

You might consider taking your game to new heights. Literally.

There are several factors that determine how far the same golf ball hit by the same club off a tee set at the same height will actually travel. The swing is one. The turf is another; its hardness, softness, and cut all impact on how the ball rolls after landing. We'd all gain distance if fairways were paved over as parking lots and cartpaths. The swing, the ball, the tee, and the turf can all be controlled and made to repeat anywhere.

What can't be controlled, on any given day, is the air the ball must fly through — and if you're hitting a ball 250 yards, it can be safely assumed you're getting it up in the air.

The temperature and density of that air are the two key variables that the USGA takes into account in the formula it uses to come up with a standard model of ball flight. Given the constants of swing, ball, tee, and turf, the formula determines (give or take ten yards) how far your drive should travel any place on earth.

So, say your home club is at sea level, the temperature is about seventy degrees, and no wind is blowing. On a decent day, the air's barometric pressure — which is related to its density— would read about thirty inches of mercury. In those conditions, the drive you hit 250 yards in the air would be traveling about ninety-five feet per second — roughly sixty-five miles per hour — hitting the ground at a thirty-six-degree angle. Air density determines the ball's lift, flight, and landing patterns. Depending on the turf conditions, it would then roll anywhere between ten and thirty-four more yards. A leonine effort, to be sure, but still no Tiger.

Now take those exact same constants to Tuctu Golf Club in Morococho, Peru, on a windless, seventy-degree day. At 14,335 feet above sea level, Tuctu is the highest-altitude course in the world, and in its less-dense atmosphere — the barometer would be reading about seventeen and a half inches of mercury there — your ball's flight would be quite different. The air's thinness would translate into less lift at launch, so despite less resistance

> "IF YOU ARE GOING TO THROW A CLUB, IT IS IMPORTANT TO THROW IT AHEAD OF YOU, DOWN THE FAIRWAY, SO YOU DON'T WASTE ENERGY GOING BACK TO PICK IT UP."
> — TOMMY BOLT

from the atmosphere, your 250-yard drive at sea level would actually carry one yard less. But the ball's trajectory would be much lower, and its angle at impact much shallower — only twenty-four degrees. That means it would be landing much harder — at 140 feet per second, or about ninety-five miles per hour — in effect skidding off the turf and rolling faster and farther, before ultimately coming to rest about 330 yards from the tee. Be forewarned, though: unless you've acclimated yourself slowly, you'll most likely pass out from altitude sickness before ever letting loose with your roar.

Of course, if you really want to test your power, you might put the Kallia Golf Course in Jericho, at 1,250 feet below sea level, on your itinerary; it's the lowest-altitude track on the planet. Interestingly, with a barometer reading of just over thirty-one inches, its conditions would play surprisingly close to what you'd find at sea level. Your tee shot's lift, flight path, and landing pattern would be so similar to sea level, in fact, that despite the altitude difference, the heavier air would only impede the total distance of your drive — carry and roll — by about six yards. That's still less, though, and less off the tee is, by definition, never more.

— J.S

*188*

# Some Experiments and Observations: The Time of Flight of a Well-Hit Golf Shot

## by O. B. Keeler

*Based at the* Atlanta Journal, *Oscar Bane Keeler (1882-1950) had an extraordinary relationship with Bobby Jones. The two collaborated on the Master's first autobiography in 1927, and remained lifelong friends. Shortly after Jones won his Grand Slam in 1930, he signed a staggering $101,000 contract with Warner Brothers for twelve instructional short-subject films. Keeler worked on those films with Jones, and, in 1931, filed this report for* The American Golfer.

It was during the shooting of the seventh episode in his series, *How I Play Golf,* that Bobby Jones and I got to talking of the duration of the period of flight for a golf ball: the time it remained in the air. It was

"GOLF IS THE ONE GAME I KNOW WHICH BECOMES MORE AND MORE DIFFICULT THE LONGER ONE PLAYS IT."

— BOBBY JONES

no new topic, certainly. Long before Bobby was born — at any rate, some time in the '90s — I read an article setting out the flight period of a golf ball in a full shot from a driver as being six seconds. Well, I won't say I read that article or reference in some book in the '90s, but it must have been written then, because it was about the gutta-percha ball, which was superseded by the rubber-cored ball in 1902; the year in which Bobby Jones was born, by the way.

Anyway, we were talking about the flight time, and I asked Bobby if he had tried it, and he said yes, several times.

"It's just six seconds, for a full shot with the driver," he said.

And that was interesting. Because, of course, Bobby had tried it with the lively ball, which could be hit 30 percent or such a matter farther than the stubborn old guttie. And the duration of flight was the same for each, with the modern ball carrying 240 yards (we'll say) and the guttie around 200.

This suggested another line of thought. "Did you ever try the time for a full shot from the other clubs?" I inquired. He had not. So we tried that, during a lull in the picture shooting. I had a stopwatch in my pocket, which we used for timing movie scenes. Bobby let fly half a dozen shots with the spoon first. Shot after shot traveled out in a smooth and equable trajectory and as the ball touched the turf, an eighth of a mile away, the split-second hand of the timer was right on top of the mark for the sixth second.

"I think the ball can be made to stay up longer," said Bobby. And he hit a towering spoon shot, with a lot of spin holding up the projectile. It was up six and two-fifths seconds. "But that's not the normal full shot with the spoon," was Mr. Jones's comment. And he reached into the bag for a big iron.

The big iron shot was as far as that from the spoon, carry and roll, but not quite as far in the air. The flight-period, however, was six seconds; precisely the same.

Bobby grinned, and picked up a mashie-niblick. "We'll try a full shot now," he said. And up it buzzed, a fairly steep pitch, with a lot of backspin, and a flight of (I should say) 140 to 150 yards; more range than Mr. Jones ordinarily exacts of the mashie-niblick.

The ball touched the turf as the split-second hand touched the sixth second. Over and over again.

The bell rang then, and school "took in." So we did not try the intermediate irons or the niblick. But I think it was needless, anyway. Judged by the flight time of a full shot from the driver, the spoon, the big iron and the mashie-niblick, a golf ball struck by an expert with normal trajectory remains in the air six seconds from any club except the putter, which, of course, is not a club for making full shots. The extreme range of the niblick under normal conditions, and played as a niblick, will be only half as far as the carry from a properly struck driving shot. But the ball will consume six seconds in flight, just the same. And this apparently was true of the guttie, just as of the modern ball.

# A Game of Inches

*Golf is a game of making the most of our imperfections, and even small imperfections take their toll. One factor that affects optimum distance is the ability to make contact with the ball squarely on the center of the club face. The farther off center, the more distance is lost. Here's a breakdown on what mis-hits with a driver can cost based on studies by Alastair Cochran and John Stobbs in* The Search for the Perfect Swing:

Solid center hit  . . . . . . . 250 yards
1/4-inch off center . . . . . 245 yards
1/2-inch off center  . . . . 235 yards
3/4-inch off center . . . . . 215 yards

Beyond that, it's best not to know.

—J. S.

# In Conversation with Richard Mackenzie

*In his often-anthologized short story "Farrell's Caddie," John Updike created an almost mythic title character: a bag-toting Scotsman with the kind of vision that can lock onto a lost ball and a lost soul with equal clarity. That Updike chose to set his story in Scotland was no accident. It is golf's Magic Kingdom. We expect our guides to its green pastures to be at least part wizard and completely colorful. Richard Mackenzie, caddie manager at the most hallowed ground of all, St. Andrews, and author of* A Wee Nip at the 19th Hole, *a delightful history of his profession, meets those expectations with the easy certainty of a two-inch putt.*

JS: What separates a good caddie from a mere bag carrier?

RM: From the St. Andrews point of view the caddie comes into his own especially when the wind blows. Their skills have been handed down from one generation to another. They can give you lines off the tee, they can give you lines on the green, they can club you within a few holes of seeing your swing, whatever your abilities. They can give advice on the shot required. More importantly, a good caddie is also a companion. He can tell you the pubs to drink in. In fact, we have a pub just up from the seventeenth hole on the Old Course called the Jigger Inn, and the caddies like to say, "You jigger in and you stagger out." That's about the size of it. They're a combination of a lot of things.

JS: It's obvious from your description that you hold the tradition quite dear.

RM: Indeed. The caddie is an institution. He's part of the way of life in Scotland. He looks at himself not just as a beast of burden; his knowledge of the course is his craft.

JS: So just where do caddies come from?

RM: As far as I know, they've always been with us. In the early days there were forecaddies, and one of the first forecaddies that I can recall is Andrew Dixon, who came on the scene about 1665. He was a forecaddie for the Duke of York, who was soon to become King James.

JS: What's the difference between a caddie and a forecaddie?

RM: The forecaddies were — and still are, on some courses — used for preparing the sand-tee and handing the club to his golfer. The forecaddie then ran forward to spot where

> "THIS IS A GAME OF MISSES. THE GUY WHO MISSES THE BEST IS GOING TO WIN."
> — BEN HOGAN

the ball would land. Without this precaution the ball would quite easily be lost in the heavy gorse of the thick grass, especially on the old courses. Today's cry of "fore" is used as a word to "take care" and is an early abbreviation of the word forecaddie.

JS: You're basically telling your forecaddie to keep an eye on the ball, then?

RM: Oh yes, and sometimes they were very beneficial, although we had some caddies at St. Andrews who actually made money by running ahead of the game and losing the ball. One of them was an old character called Trapdoor. He pretended that one leg was shorter than the other; he had a special boot made with a hole in the sole, and he would work the ball into this hole in his boot and declare it lost. Although he was fined sixpence for losing the ball, he would invariably sell it back to the same golfer later on for ninepence, which makes good business.

JS: All the caddies that you send out now are human, but that wasn't always the case, was it?

RM: No, it wasn't. They didn't always have two legs —

sometimes they had four legs. Some of the early members used to take their ponies round the Old Course. One of them, in fact, employed three caddies: one to carry the clubs, one to hold the pony, and one to clean up the pony's dirt as it went round the course. The club actually introduced a rule — I think it was rule 23 — to do with loose impediments, so you can use your imagination!

JS: There were also some dog caddies in the old days, weren't there?

RM: They referred to them as dog caddies, but in fact they were actually all ball finders. They were dogs on the end of forty-yard leads, sent into the gorse bushes to search for balls. It was very lucrative then and it still is.

JS: And the dogs, unlike Trapdoor, don't hide the balls in their paws.

RM: That's not quite true. Some of the dogs were trained to have their own stashes within the gorse bushes.

JS: Are the caddies still as colorful and all-knowing as they were in the days of, say, Trapdoor?

RM: Oh, definitely. They're still with us. The modern requirement is for a much more acceptable dress code, but

"THE DIFFERENCE BETWEEN A SAND BUNKER AND WATER IS THE DIFFERENCE BETWEEN A CAR CRASH AND AN AIRPLANE CRASH. YOU HAVE A CHANCE OF RECOVERING FROM A CAR CRASH."
— BOBBY JONES

you don't change what's inside their heads. What's in there is handed down from father to son. Something that you have to remember is that caddies came from the poorer sections of the community and they were considered social outcasts. They were actually considered on a par with street cleaners or markers in billiard saloons. True caddies had this inherent belief in themselves that they were free spirits. And some of them had wonderful philosophies. In fact, to quote one of the earlier caddies, Bill Anderson, he said, "They were rich in courtesy to their golfers, which made them rich in life." Here you had this free spirit, but as soon as he took charge of the golfer's clubs, he was with his man — they were a team. It's a wonderful thing to see work.

JS: But is there a different level of professionalism now?

RM: Sure. The caddies are more aware of the need for a man to play well rather than just go around with him. All the caddies that I take aboard, especially the junior ones, are trained in every aspect of caddieing. They learn from an early age how to rake bunkers, how to stand by the pin.

They have to pass tests before moving on.

JS: When you're caddieing, what can you tell about the person by the way he or she plays?

RM: Their character and personality. The thing about golf is it exposes you. The truth comes out on the golf course.

JS: You've been at St. Andrews since the late '70s. Is it safe to assume you know the course?

RM: Only just.

# Brassie, Please:
# What's in a Name?

*In a more poetic era, golf clubs had names attached, not numbers. This is the way the old names match up to their contemporary numerical counterparts:*

Driver (a.k.a. Playclub) — Driver

Brassie — two-wood

Spoon — three-wood

Cleek — four-wood

Baffing-spoon — five-wood

Mid-iron — two-iron

Mid-mashie — three-iron

Mashie-iron (or baffie) — four-iron

Mashie — five-iron

Spade-mashie (or spade) — six-iron

Mashie-niblick — seven-iron

Pitching-niblick — eight-iron

Niblick — nine-iron

Putting cleek — putter

To make matters just a bit more complex, a one- or two-iron was sometimes called a cleek, and a three-iron could also pass as a baffie.

# 10
# DRIVE, HE SAID

(THE HOW-TO'S OF GOLF)

# Practice Doesn't Make Perfect. Perfect Practice Makes Perfect

### by Roger Maltbie

*Roger Maltbie is an NBC golf analyst and five-time winner on the PGA Tour. He is equally at home on the range, on the course, and in the booth. This excerpt is from his book,* Range Rats.

As is true for most Tour pros, I'm often asked questions about the golf swing. I don't mind at all. This is a tough game, and if I can lighten anyone's burden, I welcome the opportunity.

But when I talk with these golfers, more often than not I find that the problems they encounter have little to do with the golf swing. The problem is with the way they practice.

A man came up to me at a benefit tournament for junior golf with an exasperated look in his eyes and told me he had been playing this game for years, but he just did not seem to be getting anywhere. He needed advice on his swing, he said.

I told him that if he was looking for a magic lamp to rub, he was talking to the wrong cowboy, because I ran out of genies somewhere around my second year on Tour. But I was more than happy to help, so I asked him what he was working on in practice. He shook his head and said it must be the wrong thing.

I asked him if he had looked at his fundamentals. He half-smiled and said he had seen videos of his swing. He said his stance was all screwed up — the feet are lined up way out to the right and his shoulders dead left. But every time he tried to correct the problem the ball went all over the place and he just can't stand it anymore. He needed to start over. A whole new swing, he said. Well, I leaned back and told him his problem wasn't at all in his swing. The problem was in his practice sessions. He gave me that goofy look I always see whenever I mention the problem might be in the way a golfer practices this game.

Of course the ball goes all over the place! I told him that when any golfer works on a new position or technique in the golf swing, it always destroys rhythm and tempo. Every time.

When the practice session involves learning a new position, the goal is not where the ball goes. The goal is learning a new position, creating a new habit. I say it takes a fig-

> "MOST GOLFERS PREPARE FOR DISASTER. A GOOD GOLFER PREPARES FOR SUCCESS."
> — BOB TOSKI

urative "twenty-one days" to learn a new position, to create a new habit in the golf swing. For twenty-one days you simply cannot care where the ball goes. And that is that.

I explained to him that learning a swing position (hands position, take-away, turn, etc.) was only one of two distinct kinds of practice sessions. The other practice session is all about getting your game from the practice tee to the golf course. In that session, the only concern is target and ball flight, where the ball goes. Nothing else, just target and flight.

I could tell by his lost expression that he was hearing all this for the first time. I had seen that look too many times before....

It has always bothered me how little the average golfer knows about practice. With the mountains of instructional material available to the general public, practically nothing has reached the average golfer about the most important aspect of any attempt to improve — how to practice what they're learning.

Let's start by identifying the two practice sessions in golf. I call them Practice A and Practice B. I also call Practice A "practicing golf," and I call Practice B "practicing the swing." Practice A is all about practicing the game itself, practicing golf the way it is played on the golf course. That may seem pretty straightforward at first glance, but I was on Tour a decade before I learned anything about this practice (A) session.

Practice B is the practice session golfers are most familiar with, but that does not mean they know how to do it. This type of practice is all about learning a position in the golf swing, incorporating a swing fundamental, creating a new habit. It is technical practice, mechanical practice, the kind of practice that has a golfer hitting balls well into the night, and again at daybreak.

The problem with far too many golfers is they mix up these two practice sessions. You have to know what to expect from each, how to use each....

I told my new friend that he was mixing up the two distinct practice sessions, and that was the problem. His goal was to create a new habit. But he was was gauging his progress on where the ball was going.... Practice A has to do with where the ball goes. Practice B does not.

By working on a swing position and getting frustrated with where the ball was going, he had broken the cardinal rule of serious practicing, which is keeping those two practice sessions separate.

I explained further that he had broken another rule of practice by expecting results right away. When the ball started going all over the place, he was convinced

> "THE WOODS ARE FULL OF LONG HITTERS."
> — HARVEY PENICK

he was working on the wrong thing. He gave up on his new stance and tried something else. Before he knew it he was doing guesswork, the great destroyer of all practice sessions. That is the danger. When you start practicing guesswork, you're toast.

I told him how he practiced is every bit as important as what he practiced. The contest is not the number of balls hit, it is the quality of work accomplished.... Practice doesn't make perfect. Perfect practice does....

*"That's it? 'Keep my head down'?"*

Ben Hogan was once asked what his secret really was, and he told that man to go dig it out of the ground as he had. There is a lot of truth there — to learn this game, you must practice. To play

> "YOU CAN TELL A GOOD PUTT BY THE NOISE IT MAKES."
> — BOBBY LOCKE

this game well, to play it to the best of your ability, all it takes is hard work. There's nothing that about 200 buckets of balls won't cure. LARGE buckets. Practice B.

But somewhere, at some unspecified point in time, we lost track of our priorities. Hit a thousand balls the wrong way and you've accomplished nothing. Indeed, you may have grooved a mistake....

Particularly if you've mixed up Practice A with Practice B.

So. What constitutes a good practice? It depends. But let me tell you a story. It's about Practice A.

One morning at the Hawaiian Open, Lee Trevino had overslept and showed up late for practice. He was teeing off in just a few minutes. So he's running down to the range saying he is late and telling no one in particular that he's got to get going. Then he takes an open spot next to Tom Watson.

Watson says, "OK, Mex, show me something."

Lee had not hit a ball yet, not one shot. He was still tying his shoes.

"What do you need to see?" Lee inquired.

And Watson said, "Hit the 100-yard sign."

"Give me something tough. That's too easy. Tell you what. I'll hit the right zero," Trevino chirped.

Everybody's watching by this time.

"To do that, though, to hit that right zero, I'm going to have to knock it down and turn it over a little bit right to left," he said.

His first shot hit smack in the middle of that right zero on the 100-yard sign. The players on the practice tee stood silently, thunderstruck, as if they had just witnessed some improbable event, like the sinking of the *Titanic*. Writ large on every countenance were the words, "Did... you... see... that?"

"It doesn't take long to warm up a Rolls Royce," Lee hollered over his shoulder as he trotted off to the putting green. His only practice warm-up was that 100-yard wedge.

There you have it.

Perfect practice does indeed make perfect.

# In Conversation with Raymond Floyd

*One of the fiercest competitors in golf history, Raymond Floyd is also acknowledged to be one of the game's smartest players. His record speaks for itself: twenty-two victories on the PGA Tour including a pair of PGA titles, a Masters championship, a U.S. Open crown at forty-three, and becoming the first player ever to win tournaments on both the PGA and Senior circuits in the same season. Much of that success comes from Floyd's ability to score well even when he's not playing particularly well, an absolute must for success on the golf course.*

JS: You like to make the distinction between just playing the game and getting the most from the game. What is that exactly?

RF: Let's put it this way: You wouldn't go out to play baseball, hit the ball and run to third base. That's not playing the game properly. So why do people go out to golf and not play it properly? Part of the proper playing of the game is to shoot the lowest score you can or be the best you can be. It's knowing how to play the game.

JS: How do you get the most from your game?

RF: I tell people to play comfortable and only play the shots that they're comfortable with. Don't try to hit a ball through the tree over the creek. Go ahead and chip the thing out. The final result is the lowest score, not the one heroic shot that you pulled off, because for every one of those, you're going to have ten that you weren't lucky with, and it's going to add two strokes or three strokes a hole to your score.

JS: So many golfers seem to have a misguided conception of the quality of their own games. Because we can hit an occasional terrific seven-iron 155 yards and have it stop two feet from the pin, we think every one of our seven-irons will do that. How does your "comfortable" concept apply to that?

RF: Playing comfortable is knowing how far you hit a club realistically. The biggest fault that I see playing in pro-am events week-in and week-out is that so many people underclub by thinking that it's going to be the perfect shot every time. Playing comfortable is not forcing yourself to hit the perfect shot. Any time you have to hit a perfect shot,

> "YOU MUST WORK VERY HARD TO BECOME A NATURAL GOLFER."
> — GARY PLAYER

there is much more pressure. Then the mental anxiety comes in, and you're less apt to hit the perfect shot.

> "PLAY WITH A CONTROLLED MAD."
> — SAM SNEAD

JS: Golfers are relatively smart people. Why are we all so delusional about our games and our abilities?

RF: People play golf in a reckless way. They know that at some point they've hit this great shot, and there's a little hole through those trees, and they think, "I might as well give it a chance because I'm only going to get to play golf once this week." So they make a quadruple bogey on the hole, where I really believe it would have been much more satisfying to chip the ball out and make a par that way playing smart.

JS: What are your basic suggestions for the man or woman who gets to play once a week, maybe less, and wants to improve? What are the fastest ways that they can begin thinking more professionally on the course?

RF: A golfer must find a pre-shot routine, because once you learn a routine — and it doesn't matter what it is — it becomes automatic. It's a golfer's automatic pilot. It sets you in motion. It starts things flowing at the right pace.

JS: When do you begin your pre-shot routine?

> "TODAY YOU DRIVE UP TO THE AVERAGE COUNTRY CLUB PRACTICE AREA AND SEE ABOUT THREE DINOSAURS FOR EVERY GOLFER WHO'S OUT THERE WORKING ON PITCH-AND-RUN SHOTS."
>
> — LEE TREVINO

RF: At twenty or thirty yards away from the ball, you should be hearing the birds sing or smelling the grass that was just mowed or talking to your friend or enjoying the ambience of where you are. Part of the enjoyment of the game of golf is your surroundings. The golf is played for only about twenty seconds per shot. That's when you have to think, get a yardage, figure what shot suits the yardage and what club it takes to get there. Then you get behind the ball, start your pre-shot routine, go through it and hit the shot. After that, you've got to enjoy your walk again, and enjoy your surroundings. I've heard people say, "All right, I'm gonna really concentrate today. Now, don't talk to me." Well, they're dead! You can't concentrate for four hours. That's not golf.

JS: Golf is a game of great frustrations. How do you deal with that, and how do you suggest we deal with it?

RF: We all deal with it in different ways. Again, I think golf is a game that's taken way too seriously, and people expect way too much out of themselves. Let's take it as a game and take it a little lighter. If you miss, you miss. Just see how good you can do from here on.

JS: So, I'm standing on the first tee with you, ready to hit. What do you tell me?

RF: If I see you're nervous, something like, "Swing hard in case you hit it."

JS: A psychological trick to take the pressure off?

RF: Sure.

JS: There's a remarkable intensity — a glare in your eyes — when you're on the course. There's nothing like it on the tour. Where did that come from?

RF: I've heard about it. I've seen it in replay. That's my focus when I am really hooked in. I am so into what I'm doing and so comfortable, it's like I'm out somewhere else. I know my steps are lighter. I feel more like I'm gliding, not really walking. That's when the club and the body are one and the same. I think all athletes at their highest level achieve this in some sense. And that's where I am when you see that glare. And even though that glare is there I'm very comfortable and enjoying my surroundings.

JS: Is there a shot you know you can always rely on?

RF: Every player will tell you if you ask what's his best shot: "If you had to do something for all the money, how would you play it?" A top player, even though he'll skirt the issue, if you asked if he had one shot to execute for a million dollars, what would that shot be? — he's gonna tell you a specific shot: a high hook, a low fade, a knock-down.

JS: For a million dollars, I like those one-inch putts!

RF: Well, you know, I've always said the easiest shot in golf is the fourth putt!

# School Daze: Why I Headed to the Desert to Search for a Swing

### *by Jeff Silverman*

Thwack...

Thwack...

Thwack...

Thwack...

The sound is resonant and it is heavenly, the perfect sound of the perfect hit. It echoes explosively at impact, then hums, almost soothingly, as the club face brushes through the grass. It is Zen-like, this sound; there is harmony in the yins and yangs of its cosmic contradiction.

And mostly, it is a sound that *other* golfers make. The sound of my swing is different; through decades of golfing despair, it has reflexively added components like wails of woe and undeleted expletives.

Ah, but…

Thwack…

Is this *me?*

Thwack…

I am standing in the midst of the Arizona desert undergoing a certified out-of-body experience. Launching six-irons toward the peaks of the McDowell Mountains straight ahead, I am hitting straight, and I am hitting long, and I am hearing that wonderful sound from an unaccustomed vantage point: its maker.

Thwack…

Its consistency is thrilling…

Thwack…

… and it has me unglued.

Nothing *feels* right. Not my grip, not my stance, not the plane of my swing, or its rhythm; all have been overhauled on this first morning of three days of focused instruction by the professionals — Gary McCord and Peter Kostis — whose names surround the slash of the Kostis/McCord Learning Center at the Grayhawk Golf Club on the northern fringe of Scottsdale.

Of course, an overhaul is just what my swing — a few quarts low from the get-go — needed. Indeed, an overhaul is precisely what I wandered into the desert for. But I wasn't quite ready for *this.*

"FOCUS ON REMEDIES, NOT FAULTS."
— JACK NICKLAUS

Hands-on in the literal sense, Kostis and McCord

have pushed me and pried me and bent me out of shape to the point that my muscle memory, built up over a lifetime of bad habits, has segued directly through Alzheimer's into something of a second child-

"OF ALL THE HAZ-ARDS, FEAR IS THE WORST."
— SAM SNEAD

hood. The success is unnerving. I keep waiting for the dissonant thumps to return.

Thwack...

I glance over my shoulder for some assurance that this game hasn't finally separated me from my marbles entirely. Kostis, golf guru extraordinaire, rocks back on his heels enigmatically, his arms folded across his chest. He has seen golf-induced hysteria before. His nod is economic and comforting.

"But," I carp, because carping is a golfer's birthright, "it doesn't feel like I'm *swinging.*"

"Let me contradict you," he barks, his glare in my face like a drill sergeant's. "You just *swung* a club for the first time. You were completely incapable of hitting these shots twenty-four hours ago."

Or, for that matter, twenty-four minutes ago.

It's a miracle.

Thwack...

I believe.

Oh, Lord, do I believe...

\* \* \*

219

Of this I am sure: the gods of golf have never liked me.

Somewhere between conception and birth, they implanted in me a latent obsession for the game that would lie dormant until both mind and body had wobbled into middle age, the better to assure that the tempered grace of the perfect swing would remain forever beyond my reach. Still, they teased me with hope, these gods; golf *kills* you with hope. From round to round, they allowed just the requisite number of decent shots — and even the occasional great one — to keep me going. I could live with that.

What I was no longer willing to live with was the rueful realization that had I not misspent my youth opting to ponder the essential Ben Jonson instead of the essential Ben Hogan I'd be a happier, more contented man today. Lord Byron's mechanics? *Those* I understand, and where do they get me from a greenside bunker? It was Byron *Nelson's* I should have dedicated myself to.

So there I stood, mired on the dark side of life's mid-point, saddled with a game of flubs and foozles. Face-to-face with the dogleg in the road, I decided to go to golf school.

I chose the three-day session at Kostis/McCord because the price was reasonable and the setting was superb. Its promise of no more than four students to a teacher was par for the course, and it provided all the requisite gizmos and video equipment that golfers cling to like security blankets.

And it had Peter Kostis and Gary McCord.

In the golf world, their reputations and personalities precede them. They are kind of like the Abbott and Costello of golf pros, except that the shorter one, Kostis, is the straight man. Both are colorful commentators on CBS's golf broadcasts.

Together, they pooled what they knew and their abilities to communicate it, and hung out their shingle at Grayhawk in 1995. It was no contest; I would be malleable putty in their hands.

> "I NEVER HIT A SHOT, NOT EVEN IN PRACTICE, WITHOUT HAVING A VERY SHARP, IN-FOCUS PICTURE OF IT IN MY HEAD."
> — JACK NICKLAUS

\* \* \*

Thursday morning, 8:15 a.m. I am fifteen minutes early for class.

A small mountain of balls dumped into miniature golf bags await me and my two classmates at the school's practice area. All of them beckon, "Hit me."

I reach for my driver, but prudence dictates I pull out a wedge. Taking aim at a huge net some seventy yards away, I put every bit of effort I have into lofting the ball neatly into its perimeter, my first mistake of the morning. I cringe as I watch the ball hug the earth, dribbling away anemically.

From behind me, I hear McCord's unmistakable voice, "Ball a little heavy today?" Yeah, Gary. About as heavy as my heart.

Kostis and McCord have somehow materialized out of

the thin desert air — a trick they will continually perform — and have been quietly studying our hitting for a few minutes.

Kostis begins simply. "There's no set system here," he announces. "There is no set program." I start to worry — I need a system; I need a program. "The message," he continues, "is that there is no message." Panic sets in; I need a message, too. "Everything we want to do we want to try and apply to each of you individually." OK. I'm inhaling again.

Their aim, he swears, is to help us each learn the fundamentals that will allow us to find our own best swing. "This is not," he says, his voice as smooth as a three-foot putt with no break, "an assembly line."

Then he asks me if I could fix one thing about my game, what it would be; I say consistency. "I can hit the shots," I say, "just not on anything that resembles a regular basis."

"No one else can either," Peter assures me. "Anyway, golf is all about the quality of your bad shots. It's a game of 'how can I control *when* and *how* I mis-hit the ball.'" Kostis is beginning to work on our heads as well as our mechanics.

As McCord stands in front of us gracefully not mis-hitting a seven-iron — "I'm just an incredible hitting machine," he smiles — Kostis offers a basic lesson in physics. "If there's one thing we have to understand, it's how to propel this thing." Suddenly, McCord breaks his rhythm and pantomimes trying to lift the ball into the air the way I do. He tops it. The next shot, he over-compensates, digging under it by six inches. I've done that, too.

"Now watch this," Kostis instructs. He drops the ball to the ground and steps on it, exerting pressure on the back of the ball to spin it. It pops up. He tells us about the grooves on a golf club and the friction they create with the back of the ball. "Not understanding that" — that the ball is launched by the club hitting down on it, not our effort to lift it — "leads to every one of our mistakes."

Before we hit another ball, Kostis takes us through a primer in swing mechanics with McCord, behind him, putting words into action. Slowly, they build a full swing up from what Kostis calls "the mini-swing," a concept we will learn to hold onto like the Grail. They make it sound — and look — so damned easy.

"We call it effortless power," Kostis explains. "When a golf swing happens in the right proportion, it doesn't look like it's happening at all. Nothing looks like it's being strained, but the ball explodes off the club face. What do average golfers do? Powerless effort. Muscles get tight and their swing" — as McCord demonstrates — "looks like one big isometric exercise." Just like mine.

After a short break, I go back to my station and chunk a few. Kostis approaches. He rips the cigar from my mouth. "Concentrate on *that*," he says, pointing to the ball. I glare at him. He offers his hand. I take it, firmly; no hard feelings. "Use that handshake for business," he scoffs, returning it with a fish. "*That's* the pressure you need to grip the golf club."

Then they begin to break me down.

Every few swings, either Kostis or McCord makes a shift in

> "THERE ARE TIMES
> WHEN A GOLFER MUST
> TAKE THIS GAME BY THE
> SCRUFF OF THE NECK
> AND GIVE IT A GOOD,
> HARD SHAKE."
> — BILLY CASPER

my grip, my stance — McCord actually kicked my feet into position — my tempo, the way I take the club back, and the way I bring it forward.

"Sometimes," Kostis would tell me later, "you have to make several changes for one to work."

For the next half hour, with their constant encouragement, I keep skulling, shanking, hooking and slicing, but they won't let me get discouraged, nor will they let me return to my old habits; at one point, they even have me swinging with my back to the target to force my wrists into the shot. When Kostis calls me over to the videotape machine — his Caddie Cam — that has been preserving my hits and misses for posterity, I'm thoroughly discouraged. Until I see the monitor. As bad as all the changes in my swing feel, the swing itself looks, well, almost beautiful.

And then, finally — thwack — I sail one off my six-iron perfectly toward the mountains. Sometimes, says Kostis, that's all it takes. "Just that one little shot that you'd never hit before. It says, 'OK, I can do it. That's the plum. That's the motivation.'" I hit another, and another, and another. The feeling becomes more natural. The cursing stops. God, this is fun...

Until I wormburn the next, and pour out an expletive. I go to set up again, using my old grip and stance out of habit. Kostis smiles. "Golf is the sport that makes players greediest fastest," he warns me. "You can revert, or you can stick with it. It's up to you." I stick.

Thwack.

After lunch, Kostis and McCord take us through the rudiments of the short game — pitching, chipping, and sand play. When we break at 4 p.m., we head back to the clubhouse for beers and bull with our teachers. I'm exhausted. My hands hurt. My eyelids are drooping.

I can't wait to do it all again tomorrow.

# The Cleverest Tip

Month after month, the pages of golf magazines are filled with instructional drills that require so much fantasizing that in trying to keep them straight you just might lose sight of the game:

• To keep aim and alignment correct, imagine you're setting up on a set of railroad tracks, your feet on one, the ball on another;

• To insure the compactness of your swing, imagine your arms are tied, and your lower body confined to a phone booth or barrel;

• To keep your arms close to your body, imagine tossing a medicine ball;

• To improve weight transfer in the legs, try to clang an imaginary pair of cymbals attached to your knees;

• To get better extension past the point of impact, imagine your club's an ax, and you're chopping a tree;

• To maintain firm wrists in chipping, imagine they're in a cast;

• To help escape from bunkers, imagine a parachute softly landing the ball on the green;

• To figure the break in a long putt, imagine spilling a pail of water, then watch the way the imaginary contents run.

All of that's fine — for somebody. But what happens if you're no good at imagining stuff? Try a potato chip; it'll cure a host of swing problems. Simply pretend you're swinging with a potato chip between your teeth. If you break it, you're swinging too hard. Still can't visualize? Then bring a family-size bag of the real thing to a practice area and start working through it with your clubs. When you can swing without biting down — especially, suggests Gary McCord, with your wedges and short irons — your tempo, mechanics, and focus will be as in synch as the insides of an old pocket watch, which you won't have to visualize at all. —J. S.

# In Conversation with Curt Schilling

*With a World Series shutout and an All-Star Game start on his card, Schilling, the hard-throwing Phillie, has been one of the premiere National League pitchers of his generation. He's also a serious golfer, approaching the game with the same kind of studiousness he takes to the mound.*

JS: Why are so many baseball players attracted to golf?

CS: Using a personal perspective, I can say golf and pitching are probably as similar as any two activities in sports.

JS: How so?

CS: First, there are no external elements in pitching — nothing happens until you throw the baseball. The game doesn't begin. The game doesn't proceed. Nothing. It's very much the same in golf. Nothing happens until you swing the golf club. The parallels that stem from that are huge attractions, at least for me.

JS: What are some of those parallels?

CS: The key to both activities is repetition, and I don't think that's truer in any sport than in golf.

JS: You're talking about things like the consistency of your throwing motion and the consistency of your swing?

CS: They both have to be repeatable — and second nature.

JS: What other parallels do you find?

"THE BALL SITS THERE AND SAYS, 'NOW, IDIOT, DON'T HIT ME IN THE HAZARD. DON'T HIT ME OVER THERE, HIT ME ON THE GREEN. YOU THINK YOU CAN, IDIOT? I DOUBT IF YOU CAN. ESPECIALLY WHEN YOU'RE CHOKING YOUR GUTS OUT.'"
— DAVIS LOVE III

CS: The preparation that goes into both. When I'm playing regularly I go out with yardage books and as much information as I can. I try never to hit a shot unprepared.

JS: You pitch the same way. You're known for keeping computer files of hitters and their tendencies, and thinking out your game before you've pitched it.

"IF YOU'RE FIVE OVER WHEN YOU HIT THIS TEE, IT'S THE BEST PLACE IN THE WORLD TO COMMIT SUICIDE."
— LEE TREVINO ON THE SIXTH AT PEBBLE

CS: I never want to be surprised.

JS: But one of the realities of sports is that sometimes you are surprised. Preparation aside, there are days your fast ball doesn't pop.

CS: Golf and pitching are games of mistake management. Even the best golfers will tell you that on any day they hit only a handful of shots exactly the way they wanted. On my best day, I might feel like I'm making great pitches, but I'll only throw maybe fifteen to twenty exactly where and how I wanted them. The rest is managing your mistakes. I think too many golfers overlook the fact that they could better their game by I don't know how many shots just through preparation. For me that also includes club selection and how I put my bag together before a round. For the most part I don't carry a driver because I don't feel I'm going to run into a hole any place on earth that I can't reach in two. So putting a driver in my hand isn't giving me the best chance to succeed; it's too erratic. I carry four wedges instead, because the toughest shots for me are inside 150 yards, and in most par fours I can get myself within 150 yards off the tee with my three-wood.

JS: All right, we've established you've got power off the tee, and, with back-to-back 300-strikeout seasons, power on the mound. But what about the transition from power to finesse? When we first pick up a golf club, we want to see how far we can hit it.

CS: (laughing) And that never changes.

JS: But, over time, we do have to make compensations.

CS: Of course. You spend your life as a young man thinking that testosterone thought: the harder the better. When I started playing golf, my overriding thought swinging the golf club was "I'm gonna crush this ball." And then you end up understanding in golf, as in pitching, location is everything. It doesn't matter how hard you're throwing if you can put the ball in a spot where no one can hit it. In golf, if I can get the ball on the green in regulation with a makable putt it doesn't matter how hard I hit.

# 11

# FICTIONAL FESCUE

(THE GAME OF GOLF IN LITERATURE)

# The Only Two
# Acceptable Theories

### *by Ron Shelton and John Norville*

*Arguably the best golf movie ever made,* Tin Cup *charts the remarkable odyssey of Roy "Tin Cup" McAvoy from driving range pro in the scrubs of Texas to the U.S. Open leaderboard. In this scene "Tin Cup," played by Kevin Costner, imparts the essence of his wisdom to a new pupil, played by Rene Russo. It's a golf scene, sure, but it's also a love scene — between the players and the game. Thus beginneth the lesson:*

### TIN CUP

The first thing you gotta learn about this game, Doc, is it ain't about hitting a little white ball into some yonder hole. It's about inner demons and self-doubt and human frailty and overcoming all that crap. So... what kinda doctor'd you say you were?

### MOLLY

I'm a psychologist. In layman's terms call me a neo-Jungian, post-modern Freudian, holistic secularist.

*234*

TIN CUP

Damn.

*SHE BEGINS UNPACKING ONE OF HER BAGS, pulling out every golf gimmick on the market — swing aid straps to pull your elbows together, a ball pendulum that hangs from your hat, a metal contraption for your feet, etc.*

MOLLY

Inner demons and human frailty are my life's work. I used to practice in El Paso but I've moved here now...

TIN CUP

What're those?

MOLLY

I ordered these from the Golf Channel.

*HE STARES IN DISBELIEF as she tries to wriggle into some of this stuff. He's enchanted and dismayed.*

TIN CUP

That stuff's a waste of money.

MOLLY

I'm sure there are excesses and repetitions here, but I believe in the gathering of knowledge and I figured, well,

*235*

> "RETIRE TO WHAT? I'M A GOLFER AND A FISHERMAN. I'VE GOT NO PLACE TO RETIRE TO."
> — JULIUS BOROS

there must be some truths about the golf swing illustrated by these devices — and that you'd help me sort through it.

*SHE STANDS THERE with contraptions coming from every limb.*

MOLLY (continued)
I have dozens of golf videotapes too... and a golf watch.

TIN CUP (irritated, impatient)
Take it off. All of it. Now! You're a smart woman, for chrissakes, don't you know the work of charlatans when you see it?

*SHE DEPOSITS ALL THE GOLF GIMMICK devices in a pile.*

MOLLY
No. I can always tell when someone is lying to himself, but I'm quite susceptible and frequently wrong when that person lies to me.

(pointing to the pile of devices)
That stuff cost me over $200...

                    TIN CUP
Then it's $200 of shit...


*HE TEES A BALL, hands Molly her driver and steps back.*


                TIN CUP (continued)
Go ahead. Take a swing.


*MOLLY TAKES A PITTY-PAT SWING and whiffs, and mut-*
*ters under her breath with the ease of a longshoreman.*


                    MOLLY
Aw, fuck...


                    TIN CUP
Well you talk like a golfer...


*MOLLY UNLOADS A MIGHTY SECOND SWING. The*
*club head bounces off the mat. The ball sits untouched.*


                    MOLLY
Shit.


                    TIN CUP
"Fuck"... "Shit"... These are highly technical golf terms
and you're using them on your first lesson — this is promis-
ing.


                    *237*

MOLLY

Awright, wiseass, show me.

*TIN CUP TAKES THE CLUB from Molly, motions for her to step back, tees up a ball, and rockets a drive into the night.*

TIN CUP

Something like that.

*HE HANDS HER back the club and tees up another ball. Molly just looks at him.*

MOLLY

Impressive. Y'know, I tend to process things verbally. Can you break down into words how you did that?

*TIN CUP TAKES a deep breath — this is his speech:*

TIN CUP

"What is the golf swing?" — by Roy McAvoy.

(beat)

The golf swing is a poem. Sometimes a love sonnet and sometimes a Homerian epic, it is organic and of a piece, yet it breaks down into elegant stanzas and quatrains. The critical opening phrase of this song is the grip, in which the thumbs and index fingers of each hand form "V" shapes that must each point to the appropriate armpit, the back of each hand pointing in opposite directions but on line to the intended target, the club gripped with the fingers lightly, the small finger of the right hand overlapping the index and middle fingers of the left, with the exception of the Harry Vardon interlock, which we will not go into here tonight...

                    MOLLY (to herself)
Thank God...

*BUT HE'S OFF on a roll, lost in, well, poetry.*


                         TIN CUP
Tempo is everything, perfection unobtainable. The golfer's signature is a nod to the Gods that he is fallible...


                         MOLLY
A nod to the Gods?


                         TIN CUP
Yes... the hands cocked on the takeaway just before the weight shift pulled by the powers of the earth — it's alive, this swing, a living sculpture — down through contact with terra firma, striking the ball crisply, with character — a tuning fork goes off in your heart, your balls — such a pure feeling is the well-struck golf shot.
                                            *(beat)*
And then the follow-through to finish, always on line, the

reverse "C" of the Golden Bear, the steelworker's power and brawn of Carl Sandburg's Arnold Palmer, the da Vinci of Hogan, every finishing position unique, as if that is the brushstroke left to the artist, the warrior athlete who, finally and thereby, has asserted his oneness with and power over the universe through willing the golf ball to go where he wants and how and when, because that is what the golf swing is about...

*(finally)*

It is about gaining control of your life, and letting go at the same time.

*MOLLY STARES BACK, exhausted and intrigued.*

### MOLLY

Jeez Louise...

### TIN CUP

There is only one other acceptable theory of how to hit a golf ball.

### MOLLY

I'm afraid to ask. What's the other theory?

### TIN CUP

Grip it and rip it.

# Unshaken by Goldfinger, Bond Puts on a Stirring Display

### *by Ian Fleming*

*Journalist, banker, and spymaster, Fleming (1908-1964) also was a fine golfer. At the time of his death, he was in line to become captain of Royal St. George's, one of the venerable clubs on the British Open rotation; he suffered his fatal heart attack at a committee meeting in the clubhouse. Fleming wrote the first of his fourteen James Bond novels in 1953; six years later, in* Goldfinger, *he put 007's skills on the course to the test in a remarkable match against his formidable foe, set at the fictional St. Mark's, an obvious St. George's stand-in. The match would go down to the final hole, where Bond, champion of decency, would uphold the rules of the game and exit victorious. Winning by a technicality, he outwitted an opponent who had played a little too fast and a little too loose with those sacred rules. Here we see how one of golf's best fictional head-to-heads tees off.*

Bond paid his green-fee to Hampton, the steward, and went into the changing room. It was just the same — the same tacky smell of old shoes and socks and last summer's sweat. Why was it a tradition of the most famous golf clubs that their standard of hygiene should be that of a Victorian private school? Bond changed his socks and put on the battered old pair of nailed Saxones. He took off the coat of his yellowing black-and-white hound's-tooth suit and pulled on a faded black wind-cheater. Cigarettes? Lighter? He was ready to go.

Bond walked slowly out, preparing his mind for the game. On purpose he had needled this man into a high, tough match so that Goldfinger's respect for him should be increased and Goldfinger's view of Bond — that he was the type of ruthless, hard adventurer who might be very useful to Goldfinger — would be confirmed. Bond had thought that perhaps a 100-pound Nassau would be the form. But $10,000! There had probably never been such a high-stakes game in history — except in the finals of American Championships or in the big amateur Calcutta Sweeps where it was the backers rather than the players who had the money on... So be it. But one thing was certain, for a hundred reasons Bond could not afford to lose.

He turned into the shop and picked up the balls and tees from Alfred Blacking.

"Hawker's got the clubs, sir."

Bond strolled out across the 500 yards of shaven seaside turf that led to the first tee. Goldfinger was practicing on the putting green. His caddie stood nearby, rolling balls to him. Goldfinger putted in the new fashion — between his legs with a mallet putter. Bond felt encouraged. He didn't believe in the system. He knew it was no good practicing himself. His old hickory Calamity Jane had its good days and its bad. There was nothing to do about it. He knew also that the St. Mark's practice green bore no resemblance, in speed or texture, to the greens on the course.

Bond caught up with the limping, insouciant figure of his caddie who was sauntering along chipping at an imaginary ball with Bond's blaster. "Afternoon, Hawker."

"Afternoon, sir." Hawker handed Bond the blaster and threw down three used balls. His keen sardonic poacher's face split in a wry grin of welcome. "How've you been keepin', sir! Played any golf in the last twenty years? Can you still put them on the roof of the starter's hut?" This referred to the day when

> "THE MOST EXQUISITELY SATISFYING ACT IN THE WORLD OF GOLF IS THAT OF THROWING A CLUB. THE FULL BACKSWING, THE DELAYED WRIST ACTION, THE FLOWING FOLLOW-THROUGH, FOLLOWED BY THAT UNIQUE WHIRRING SOUND, REMINISCENT ONLY OF A FLOCK OF PASSING STARLINGS, IS WITHOUT PARALLEL IN SPORT."
> — HENRY LONGHURST

Bond, trying to do just that before a match, had put two balls through the starter's window.

"Let's see." Bond took the blaster and hefted it in his hand, gauging the distance. The tap of the balls on the practice green had ceased. Bond addressed the ball, swung quickly, lifted his head and shanked the ball almost at right angles. He tried again. This time it was a dunch. A foot of turf flew up. The ball went ten yards. Bond turned to Hawker, who was looking his most sardonic. "It's all right, Hawker. Those were for show. Now then one for you." He stepped up to the third ball, took his club back slowly and whipped the club head through. The ball soared 100 feet, paused elegantly, dropped eighty feet onto the thatched roof of the starter's hut and bounced down.

Bond handed back the club. Hawker's eyes were thoughtful, amused. He said nothing. He pulled out the driver and handed it to Bond. They walked together to the first tee, talking about Hawker's family.

Goldfinger joined them, relaxed, impassive. Bond greeted Goldfinger's caddie, an obsequious, talkative man called Foulks whom Bond had never liked. Bond glanced at Goldfinger's clubs. They were a brand new set of American Ben Hogans with smart St. Mark's leather covers for the woods. The bag was one of the stitched black leather holdalls favored by American pros. The clubs were in individual cardboard tubes for easy extraction. It was a pretentious outfit, but the best.

"Toss for honor?" Goldfinger flicked a coin.

"Tails."

It was heads. Goldfinger took out his driver and unpeeled a new ball. He said, "Dunlop 65. Number One. Always use the same ball. What's yours?"

"Penfold. Hearts."

Goldfinger looked keenly at Bond. "Strict Rules of Golf?"

"Naturally."

"Right." Goldfinger walked onto the tee and teed up. He took one or two careful, concentrated practice swings. It was a type of swing Bond knew well — the grooved, mechanical, repeating swing of someone who had studied the game with great care, read all the books and spent 5,000 pounds on the finest pro teachers. It would be a good, scoring swing which might not collapse under pressure. Bond envied it.

Goldfinger took up his stance, waggled gracefully, took his club head back in a wide slow arc and, with his eyes glued to the ball, broke his wrists correctly. He brought the club head mechanically, effortlessly, down and through the ball and into a rather artificial, copybook finish. The ball went straight and true about 200 yards down the fairway.

It was an excellent, uninspiring shot. Bond knew that Goldfinger would be capable of repeating the same swing with different clubs again and again round the eighteen holes.

Bond took his place, gave himself a lowish tee, addressed the ball with careful enmity and, with a flat, racket-player's swing in which there was just too much wrist for safety, lashed the ball away. It was a fine, attacking drive that landed past Goldfinger's ball and rolled on fifty yards. But it had had a shade of draw and ended on the edge of the left-hand rough.

They were two good drives. As Bond handed his club to Hawker and strolled off in the wake of the more impatient Goldfinger, he smelled the sweet smell of the beginning of a knock-down-and-drag-out game of golf on a beautiful day in May with the larks singing over the greatest seaside course in the world.

# On the First Tee With Rabbit Angstrom

## by John Updike

*In essays and fiction, Updike has written thrillingly about golf. As a player himself, his perspective is both blissful and pained. It's a perspective that infuses Updike's most enduring character, Harry Angstrom, the self-same Rabbit of four novels, when we meet him in this passage from* Rabbit at Rest. *The former high school star basketballer is now fifty-five, retired, living in Florida, and gazing at the world — and down the fairway — through eye-glasses.*

And the lenses are always dusty and the things he looks at all seem tired; he's seen them too many times before. A kind of drought has settled over the world, a bleaching such as overtakes old color prints, even the ones kept in a drawer.

Except, strangely, the first fairway of a golf course before his first swing. This vista is ever fresh. There, on the tee's

"A GOLFER IS ONLY AS GOOD AS HIS HANDS."
— HENRY COTTON

earth platform, standing in his large white spiked Footjoys and blue sweat socks, drawing the long tapered steel wand of his Lynx Predator driver from the bag, he feels tall again, tall the way he used to on a hardwood basketball floor when after those first minutes his growing momentum and lengthening bounds and leaps reduced the court to childlike dimensions, to the size of a tennis court and then a Ping-Pong table, his legs unthinkingly eating the distances up, back and forth, and the hoop with its dainty skirtlike net dipping down to be there on the layups. So, in golf, the distances, the hundreds of yards, dissolve to a few effortless swings if you find the inner magic, the key. Always, golf for him holds out the hope of perfection, of a perfect weightlessness and consummate ease, for now and again it does happen, happens in three dimensions, shot after shot. But then he gets human and tries to force it, to make it happen to get ten extra yards, to steer it, and it goes away, grace you could call it, the feeling of collaboration, of being bigger than he really is. When you stand up on the first tee it is there, it comes back from wherever it lives during the rest of your life, endless possibility, the possibility of a flawless round, a round without a speck of bad in it, without a missed two-footer or a flying right elbow, without a pushed wood or pulled iron; the first fairway is in front of you, palm trees on the left and water on the right, flat as a picture. All you have to do is take a simple pure swing and puncture the picture in the middle with a ball that shrinks in a second to the size of a needle-prick, a tiny tunnel into the absolute. That would be it.

But on his practice swing his chest gives a twang of pain and this makes him think for some reason of Nelson, his son. The kid jangles in his mind. As he stands up to the ball he feels crowded but is impatient and hits it outside in, trying too hard with his right hand. The ball starts out promisingly but leaks more and more to the right and disappears too close to the edge of the long scummy pond of water....

# Ten Intriguing Golf Mysteries
## (In Order of Publication Date)

1. *Murder on the Links*, by Agatha Christie (1923)
2. *The Body in the Bunker*, by Herbert Adams (1935)
3. *Trent Intervenes*, by E. C. Bentley (1938)
4. *Death of a Low Handicap Man*, by Brian Ball (1974)
5. *Winter Rules*, by Barry Cork (1993)
6. *Local Knowledge*, by Conor Daly (1996)
7. *Back Spin (A Myron Bolitor Mystery)*,
   by Harlan Coben (1997)
8. *Nasty Breaks*, by Charlotte and Aaron Elkins (1997)
9. *The Case of the Missing Link: A Golf Mystery*,
   by Lee Tyler (1999)
10. *On a Par With Murder (Morris and Sullivan Series)*,
    by John Logue (1999)

Bonus Shot: *Mermaids on the Golf Course and Other Stories*,
by Patricia Highsmith (1985). (Only one story in the selection touches on golf, but it *is* by Patricia Highsmith.)

# 12
## THE LIST

# The List

18. Jack Nicklaus's Majors

17. The Road Hole

16. The ocean carry at Cypress Point

15. Patty Berg's Majors

14. Clubs in a bag

13. Original rules of golf

12. Tiger Woods's Masters margin

11. Byron Nelson's streak

10. Automatic qualifiers for the Ryder Cup

9. Holes a side

8. Church pews at Oakmont

7. Final round deficit made up by Arnold Palmer to win the '60 U.S. Open

6. Final round lead lost by Greg Norman in the '96 Masters

5. Ben Hogan's Fundamental Lessons

4. Bobby Jones's Grand Slam

3. Balls in a sleeve

2. Gene Sarazen's double eagle

1. Jack Nicklaus. Period.